WORK PLACES TODAY

Juriaan van Meel

Centre for Facilities Management

CONTENTS

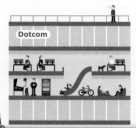

TYPE 3:
CO-WORK OFFICES 72

Co-working means working on your own, but alongside others in a shared office space. Co-working protagonists point out that the concept is not only about sharing space, but just as much about sharing a sense of community, thereby creating possibilities for synergy and collaboration.

Impact Hub 81
Amsterdam

Republikken 87
Copenhagen

Mutinerie 93
Paris

TYPE 4:
PLAY OFFICES 100

The play office is the office as playground, with bright colours, slides and foosball tables. Tech companies in particular seem to be fond of such cheerful environments. Are these offices whimsical gimmicks, or a welcome deviation from the bland efficiency of traditional office design?

Google 109
Dublin

Cisco Meraki 115
San Francisco

Lego 121
Billund

TYPE 5:
FLEX OFFICES 128

In flex offices, office workers no longer have their own desk. Instead, they share a variety of 'activity-based settings'. It is a space-saving concept that makes a lot of sense from an economic and sustainability point of view. But it is not always easy to persuade people to give up 'their' office territory.

DSM office 139
Sittard

Telenor 145
Fornebu

GlaxoSmithKline 151
Philadelphia

TYPE 6:
STUDIOS   158

Studios are spaces for creative work, where tables hold not only computers, but also models, samples, sketches, books and other creative artefacts. Studios are interesting because they are designed to foster creativity, collaboration and learning—critical qualities for any organization.

Derek Lam   167
New York

Mamastudio   173
Warshaw

MAD Architects   179
Beijing

TYPE 7:
MODERNIST
OFFICES   186

The modernist office is the classic glazed box, with neutrally coloured interiors filled with large numbers of identical desks. These offices are designed as rational machines for working in, without any ambition to be cosy, playful or trendy. They are true places for work.

Nykredit   195
Copenhagen

McKinsey   201
Hong Kong

Taikang Life   207
Beijing

TYPE 8:
PROCESS OFFICES   214

Process offices are offices where information is processed rather than produced. Think of crowded call centres and other places for 'low-end' office work. Such places are normally absent from books like this, but they are an essential part of today's digitalized economy.

Customer Service
Centre CBA   225
Melbourne

Banco Santander   231
Querétaro

Teletech   237
Dijon

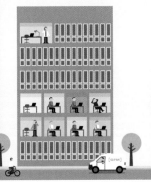

TYPE 9:
CELL OFFICES 244

Cell offices are associated with long corridors and rows of rooms. This type of office is close to extinction because it is considered incompatible with today's collaborative working ethos. Some companies, however, cling to it, seeking to create a calm environment for cognitively demanding work.

TYPE 10:
RECYCLED OFFICES 274

The office has been declared dead many times. Let's just assume those predictions do indeed come to pass. What then to do with all those empty office buildings? The most productive answer is 'adaptive re-use', giving former office buildings a new life as apartments, hotels or health care facilities.

INTRODUCTION

The term 'mobile office' was coined way back in 1969 by the Austrian architect Hans Hollein. His version of the concept, which he also dubbed a 'Transportable Studio in a Suitcase', consisted of an inflatable plastic tube connected to an electric fan. Inside the tube, which was equipped with a telephone and a drawing board, one could sit and work. It was an art installation that demonstrated Hollein's idea of the workplace in an age where new technologies would soon allow people to work anywhere and anytime, using only minimal physical space.

Since those pioneering days, a lot has been said and written about the future of the office. Numerous books have been published about the topic with enticing titles such as *The demise of the office*,[1] *The Digital Workplace: How Technology Is Liberating Work*[2] and *Undress for Success: The Naked*

Hans Hollein and his 'Mobile Office', filmed for Austrian television, 1969. The documentary showed Hollein climbing into the plastic tube while commenting, "Crazy, right?". Crazy maybe, but also visionary.

Truth about Making Money at Home.[3] Such books tend to present a bold and romantic image of the future work environment: a deskless utopia where people have escaped the tedium of the office, working from home, in cafés, or in exotic locations such as the beach or beside a pool. An editor of *The Economist* wrote in 1978: "We will be able to live in Tahiti if we want to and still be able to telecommute daily to our New York or Frankfurt or Tokyo office."[4] In retrospect, many of these predictions have proven to be too simplistic or premature. Dreams about the death of the office were fuelled by an enthusiastic belief in the power of technology, while underestimating organizational inertia and the importance of face-to-face contacts. So, despite the amazing technological advances of the past decades, the majority of today's work force still commutes back and

NEC laptop advertisement in *Personal Computing*, 1984. Claiming to have reinvented the office, it boasts that "you can take your office with you anywhere you go. On a plane, on a park bench, on the way to a meeting, or even on a beach."

forth to their offices on a daily basis, spending much of their valuable time on congested roads or in packed commuter trains. And the average office is still a soulless modernist building block, filled with standardized desks and bland meeting rooms.

Yet, at the same time, there are plenty of reasons to believe that, at last, profound changes are taking place. Just look around and you will notice that work is spilling out of the office. Using smartphones, tablets and laptops, people are working on the street, in cafés, at home, and in every other imaginable space. Work is everywhere. This has not yet resulted in the demise of the physical office, but the conventional office typology no longer has the same importance as it did in the past.

This book takes a closer look at this hybrid and transitional

Sandra Bullock in the movie *The Net*, 1995. In this shot, the movie's villain approaches Sandra Bullock, who is sitting typing on her laptop on the beach. His opening line is, "Is that business or pleasure?". "Is there a difference?" she retorts.

situation. It is not about 'the next big thing' or 'the office of the future' (there are already plenty of such books), but about the present, looking at the many different places where today's knowledge workers work. It is a typological survey that looks at ten types of workplaces that are different in terms of location, design expression, space usage, formality and the underlying intentions. It is not a rigorous or exhaustive typology, but a rather loose categorization, more journalistic than scientific in nature. The first two chapters of the book deal with 'non-office' workplace types: people's homes and public spaces such as hotels and cafés. The next three chapters explore relatively new office types: the co-work office, the play office and the flex office. They are followed by four chapters about more traditional office types that can still be considered as

Street scene in Japan, in the 1990s. The mobile office is not always so practical.

relevant: the studio, the modernist office, the process office and the cell office. The last chapter considers the 'recycled' office. Anticipating the possible demise of the traditional office, it looks into how obsolete office buildings might be used for new functions, such as hotels or housing.

By presenting a wide diversity of workplace types in one volume, the book aims to show that there is no such thing as *the* perfect workspace. There are many versions. A design studio in Warsaw has different needs from an insurance company in Beijing. Likewise, mobile workers such as sales representatives and consultants will have different preferences from more sedentary workers such as lawyers or researchers. And independent 'micro-entrepreneurs' will have different ideas about workplace design from large, established organizations with professional facility management departments. What works, or does not work, or what people believe works or does not work, depends in part on their functional demands. Just as important are 'soft' factors such as cultural norms and values, managerial ideologies and personal preferences.

The book hopes to awaken a sense of exploration and inquiry in the reader. By comparing and contrasting different types of workplaces, readers can challenge and sharpen their own thinking about work environments. It can help them to become aware that their workplace preferences, and the underlying values, are not the only ones, nor the norm. The book will demonstrate that there are many different possibilities and few limits when it comes to workplace design.

Type 1:
HOME OFFICES

Working naked. Listening to loud heavy metal. Picking the kids up early. Doing the laundry. The home office has always been an appealing option. It provides the freedom and flexibility that many office workers yearn for. But working from home can also be lonely or stressful, for example, when there are children running round. Moreover, it is still a bit of a taboo. Some managers fear it will corrode the social cohesion of their organizations. Or they have doubts about their staff's productivity at home, while staff themselves tend to argue the opposite.

From a historical point view, it can be argued that working from home is nothing new. Before the industrial revolution, craftsmen, merchants and even government officials lived and worked under one and the same roof.[5] A good illustration of this is a painting from 1627 that portrays Constantijn Huygens, a Dutch government official, casually seated at a desk in what is probably the study of his house. The messenger, the papers and the ink pot are expressions of his role as an important government official. At the same time, the scene is domestic and informal, with Huygens almost slouching on his chair next to the fireplace, surrounded by personal items such as a lute, a globe and poems.[6]

It is tempting to say that the Huygens' work environment is not so different from today's home offices. Replace the paper and the ink pot with a laptop, and think of the messenger boy as an incoming email, and the image starts to look quite familiar. It is important to acknowledge, however, that at the time the scale of organizations was small. Governments were ruled by powerful individuals. Businesses were family owned. Relations were personal and work and private life largely overlapped. This changed radically in the 19th century with the

Portrait of Constantijn Huygens and his clerk in his study, by Thomas de Keyser, dated 1627. The painting depicts Huygens in his official capacity as a public figure, but at the same time the scene is very domestic, with a fireplace and objects that reflect his personal interests, such as a lute and a globe.

emergence of the industrial revolution. Businesses grew in size and needed a large administrative apparatus to manage their operations. Office work became a specialized activity, professionally organized, taking place in environments that were specifically designed for this purpose. Work and home became disconnected and the office building became a new, dominant building type.

The modern notion of working from home (also referred to as telework, or telecommuting in the US) dates from the early 1970s. It was the American researcher Jack Nilles who coined the term 'telecommuting' in 1973. According to his own account, Nilles came up with the concept when he was stuck in traffic in Los Angeles.[7] He observed that commuting around LA was arduous, costly and time-consuming and he started thinking about ways some people might work from home or satellite offices. Backed by the National Science Foundation, he conducted an extensive study of the possibilities and concluded that telecommuting would be an excellent solution for office organizations: it would reduce costs, limit environmental pollution and increase staff productivity. With an eye for detail, he even mentioned the cost savings of not having to provide subsidized lunches in a company canteen when people work from home.[8]

Movie still from the sitcom *Sex and the City*, which started in 1998. In almost every episode, there is a scene showing columnist Carrie Bradshaw working from her Manhattan apartment, sitting in front of her laptop at a small desk, pondering the newspaper column she has to write.

Notwithstanding his enthusiasm for the concept, Nilles also mentioned its potential downsides and difficulties. He noted that people might be hesitant in embracing telecommuting because "the organization provides a significant social function for the individual; for many people the organization is their sole people-meeting place and provides their major friendship network."[9] He also noted that middle managers in particular were likely to resist the idea: "The supervisor will be threatened because apparently his or her empire is being diminished."[10] Both observations are still relevant today.

In the decades that followed, the concept of telecommuting attracted a lot of attention. Conferences were organized, books were written and large numbers of organizations experimented with the concept. Some telecommuting enthusiasts even predicted a return to pre-industrial revolution conditions. That has not happened thus far, but over the years the number of people working from home has grown steadily. The exact number and growth rate are hard to pin down. There are many different studies of the phenomenon, each using different definitions and counting methods. It can safely be argued, however, that the concept is no longer a novelty, but a mainstream phenomenon.

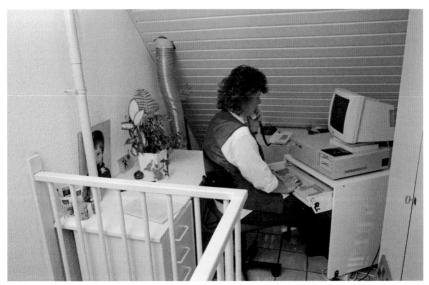

Employee of the Dutch Ministry of Infrastructure, working from home, 1990. In the 1990s, the Dutch Ministry of Infrastructure actively promoted the concept of 'telework' with the objective of reducing traffic congestion. The promotional value of this photo is obviously open to discussion.

According to the US Bureau of Labor Statistics, more than twenty per cent of employed Americans reported that they did all or some of their work at home.[11] In Europe, the adoption rate is likely to be more or less the same, although it all depends on how you define the concept.

For employees, the benefits of working from home are obvious. First and foremost, it saves them the trouble of commuting back and forth to the office. According to the advocates of teleworking, this time gain can be translated into extra working hours, and thus higher productivity. While one might seriously question the truth of this,[12] at least the absence of commuting can make people's lives easier, reducing the frustrations that may come from overcrowded commuter trains or congested roads. As one commuter put it on Twitter: "#commutingtoday - I had quickly forgotten what a waste of life and *!+* experience this is!".[13]

Another advantage for staff is that working from home can provide more flexibility to balance their work and private life. They can mix working hours with other activities such as taking children to school, working out at the gym, looking after elderly parents or children, or simply doing the shopping. It should be said, however, that there are also people who get quite stressed from such flexibility and prefer a clear-cut nine-to-five

Photo from the IKEA catalogue of 1995. The header states: "There's only one way to improve things at work. Go Home." The photo shows a smiling mother working from home, alongside her daughter who is quietly playing with paper. Reality may be rather more complicated.

work rhythm, with a physical separation between work and private life.[14] From a productivity point of view, the main benefit of working from home lies in the ability to work without the distractions of the office. There may be laundry to do, but there are no chatting co-workers, no meetings and one is spared the noise of colleagues making loud phone calls. As an IKEA advertisement for home office furniture puts it: "There is only one thing to improve things at work. Go Home." Of course, this will only be true if the house is quiet. Family members can be just as distracting as co-workers. The same IKEA advertisement shows a mother smiling benignly at her child, but she would probably look less happy if she was trying to make a business call. Interestingly, the advertisement features a woman, and not a man, suggesting that women in particular may be interested in working from home as it allows them to manage their family life at the same time—however stressful the combination may be.

One way of dealing with distractions at home is to create a separate workspace like a small room or study, away from the busy centre of the house. Most idyllic is probably a 'work shed' in one's garden. 'Shed working' is promoted as a practice that "improves work-life balance and accelerates your productivity".[15] A famous example of a shed worker

Roald Dahl working in his shed (or 'nest' as he called it) in the backyard of his house. Dahl did not use a desk because of his back problems. He worked in an old armchair that had belonged to his mother, balancing a writing board on his knees.

was Roald Dahl, the celebrated British writer of children's books. Roald Dahl wrote his books in what he called a little nest in his back yard. Only after he had closed the door of his workroom and was completely alone, could he slip into a world where his imagination took over: "I … fall into a kind of trance, and everything around me disappears. I see only the point of my pencil moving over the paper, and quite often two hours go by as though they were a couple of seconds."[16]

As the case of Roald Dahl shows, the solitude of working from home can be productive, bringing focus and concentration. But it can also be lonesome and isolated. Ordinary office workers will have different needs from writers or other independent professionals. As Nilles pointed out back in 1973, people may miss the social function of the office: the camaraderie and the 'buzz' of working with other people. Furthermore, it may not be very functional from an organizational point of view. For the individual, it is nice to be free of office distractions, but mainstream office workers tend to be part of departments or teams and have to collaborate with others. New technologies can help with this, but tweets, emails and Skype meetings can only partly replace face-to-face contact, especially those contacts that are unplanned and informal. It is for those reasons that the American management guru Thomas Davenport states that working from home will never fully replace the office. He writes: "Knowledge workers work at the office …They like flexibility, and they like to work at home occasionally. However, they know that to be constantly out of the office is to be 'out of the loop'—unable to share gossip, exchange tacit knowledge, or build social capital."[17]

Scientific evidence concerning the pros and cons of working from home are hard to come by. There are many studies available but they are often based on individual cases and the outcomes tend to be inconclusive and contradictory.[18] This makes the concept very much a topic of debate, informed by personal opinions and cultural norms and values rather than hard facts. Recently, this debate flared up again when Yahoo, the American Internet giant, decided to withdraw its long-standing work from home policy. An internal memo ("proprietary and confidential information—do not forward") from Yahoo's HR department read: "Speed and quality are often sacrificed when we work from home … We need to be one Yahoo!, and that starts with physically being together."[19] The memo asserted that it was critical for all staff to work in the office in order to increase communication and collaboration.

Almost every workplace consultant and business guru felt the urge to tweet or blog about Yahoo's policy reversal, expressing either their aversion or their understanding. Never shy of expressing an opinion, Donald Trump tweeted "@MarissaMayer (Yahoo's CEO, ed.) is right to expect Yahoo employees to come to the workplace vs. working at home. She is doing a great job!"[20] Disagreeing, the equally opinionated Richard Branson blogged: "Working life isn't 9-5 anymore. The world is connected. Companies that do not embrace this are missing a trick."[21] As so often, the truth is probably somewhere in between. Face-to-face contacts are critical for teamwork and organizational learning, while working from home may improve flexibility and productivity.

For people who work on their own, as independent freelancers or individual entrepreneurs, the Yahoo discussion appears to be less relevant. Think of independent consultants, copywriters, illustrators and other individuals who operate from their studies and kitchen tables, without managers or colleagues. For them, home is a logical place to work that is flexible, allows for tax deductions and does not cost any rent. Yet, even among these so-called SOHOs (an acronym for small offices/home offices), there is a discussion about whether it would be more productive to work in a co-work office rather than from home (see chapter 3). The advocates of co-working warn that "you can lose your edge by not being around other people" and that there is a risk of "neglecting to step outside for days at a time" when working from home.[22] Those risks are certainly real, but not for all. The home workers interviewed for this book are not hermits. Illustrator Noma Bar goes out every single day, wandering through London with his sketch book, spending time in cafés and parks to get inspiration. Likewise, investor Louise Elling spends a lot of her time visiting clients and partners and even uses friends' apartments as workplaces. For people like them, their house is an important place for work, but it is not the only place. Depending on their activities and mood, they may decide to work from home, at a café, a friend's house, the library or some other place. Having this freedom to choose where to work, may actually be the most important advantage of working from home.

Noma Bar working in the back garden of his house in London. It is mostly the production work that he does there. For generating ideas and sketching he spends lots of time in the nearby Highgate Wood.

NOMA BAR, LONDON

User: Noma Bar
Industry: art/illustration
Design and build: Ecospace Studios
Location: London
Size: 7.75 sq.m. / 75 sq.ft.
Completion: 2010

For the renowned graphic artist Noma Bar, the office is just a few steps away in the back garden of his home in central London. It is a small wooden structure that measures approximately 3 by 2.5 metres, providing just enough room for a work table, a chair and book shelves. Basically it is a garden shed, but a very comfortable one—well designed, with double-glazed windows and underfloor heating. Small as it is, it is the place where Noma produces his celebrated artworks, book covers and illustrations for newspapers like *The New York Times* and *The Guardian*.

Noma explains that he chose this solution for practical reasons: "London is extremely expensive and houses are small here. I am lucky enough to have a house with a small backyard with just enough space for a shed. The alternative would have been to rent a studio somewhere, but then I would have to commute, which takes a lot of time in London. Working from home is easier. I can bring my daughter to school at nine, and twenty minutes later I am at work."

He considers the closeness of his family as one of the main advantages of this way of working. "I see my family all the time, almost literally because I can see inside my house from my studio window. I am there when they need me. So, I can work with a clear conscience." Being close to his family does not mean, however, that he is not making long hours. On the contrary. With the rise of his fame, he has become extremely busy, with ever more deadlines. Illustration work for newspapers and magazines can be especially demanding. Smiling, he says: "Just like anybody else, I am part of the big sausage production machine, but I feel that I am on the happier side of the sausage machine."

The garden studio is not his only place of work. Most of his time is spent wandering around the city with his sketch book and laptop, working in public spaces such as cafés and parks. "I use my studio mostly for computer work, such as answering emails and making the digital versions of illustrations. The thinking, sketching and brainstorming takes place outdoors." His favourite work spot is Highgate Wood, an ancient woodland in North London, close to his home. "You can find me working there for hours, no matter the weather. Today I was sitting there with an umbrella. Raindrops were wetting my sketch book, but I love it there".

Noma explains that his work is of a solitary nature and that it is important to get out. "I need quiet, but also noise. I am actually very pleased to be distracted. When you think of something too much, you get stuck. Being out there helps to get ideas, overhearing conversations in cafés, watching people on the street, or just sitting in the park." Once ideas have taken shape, he can do the production work on his laptop in his studio.

Sometime in the future, Noma Bar would not mind having a larger studio. He recently took up sculpting and created an embossing machine shaped like a giant shiny dog. "It would be great to have the dog here and have more space for my artworks." He ponders, however, that there might be a relation between the smallness of his workspace and his minimalistic design style. Both are highly efficient and stripped down to their bare essentials, creating maximum effect with minimal means. "A large, lavish loft studio space would be nice obviously, but it's not really me." Thinking about the perfect workplace, Noma believes that a studio on wheels would probably be the best solution, allowing him to roam the world and work from anywhere.

Noma Bar's work pod is just eight square metres (75 sq.ft.) in area and comes with energy efficient, underfloor heating so that it can be used year round.

From his desk, Noma Bar can look straight into his house. Being close to his family is one of the main reasons he opted for this solution.

Home/office of Gaaga Architecture. A concrete staircase connects the ground-floor office space with the kitchen and living room on the first floor.

GAAGA ARCHITECTURE, LEIDEN

User: Gaaga Architecture
Industry: architecture
Design: Gaaga Architecture
Location: Leiden, the Netherlands
Size: 2,006 sq.m. / 2,217 sq.ft (office + house)
Completion: 2012

Gaaga Architecture is a small but acclaimed Dutch architecture practice led by two partners, Arie Bergsma and Esther Stevelink, who also happen to be partners in private life. When this couple was presented with the opportunity to build a new house in the Dutch city of Leiden, they decided to design a building that would serve as both office and home. Esther Stevelink explains: "Earlier, we rented a workspace in a multi-tenant office building in The Hague, and we were living in Delft. It was nice to work in The Hague, but traffic jams made our daily commute a nightmare. We started to look for new office space, but spaces were either too expensive or too inflexible. Most offices have lease durations longer than five years, which doesn't work for a small firm like us." This prompted the idea of creating a mixed-use residence, for which an opportunity presented itself in Leiden.

The house is located in a former industrial area that has been redeveloped as a residential area and where there was the possibility, still rare in the Netherlands, for individuals and families to design and build their own homes. The local authorities supplied a schematic urban plan based on a grid, giving the home owners a framework to fill in. Esther and Arie's house is located on one of the corner plots. It is called the Stripe House because of the horizontal stripes that are carved into the building's facade (approx. 7,000 metres of stripes, hand-carved in semi-hardened plaster).

The building is a cube-like structure containing three similarly sized floors, each of which has a different programme. The office is located on the ground floor. It is one large space with two large work tables. The interior is basic, with white walls and a light-coloured wooden floor. One wall has bookshelves along its entire length, providing plenty of room for project folders and architecture books. The work tables provide room for both Arie and Esther and the one or two interns they usually have working with them. Next to the workspace there is a separate toilet and pantry so that there is no need to make use of those in the house.

The more private, residential functions are located upstairs: a kitchen and living room on the first floor, and bedrooms on the upper floor. This vertical organization enables the Gaaga partners to keep their work and private life separate, although they are not always very strict in maintaining that separation. Esther Stevelink: "When I have to work evenings or weekends—something that is quite common in our line of business—I always go downstairs to the office. I keep all my work-related stuff there, which avoids my being constantly reminded of work." At the same time, however, Esther admits that she has sometimes held client meetings in her first-floor kitchen. "Architecture is a personal business. I see no harm in having a client meeting in my kitchen. The advantage is that I don't disturb the others who are working in the open office space downstairs. Besides, it may help to give a client ideas if, for example, we are designing a private home for them."

From an urban planning point of view, mixed-use developments like this are interesting because buildings like the Stripe House encourage the growth of small businesses that bring activity into suburban areas that would otherwise be rather dull and sleepy during the day. Furthermore, it is obvious that this type of 'zero-commute housing' helps to reduce traffic congestion and associated environmental problems. The only disadvantage may be that one's world becomes smaller. Esther Stevelink: "You're in one space most of the time. That's efficient in terms of travel time, but you can also feel a bit locked in. Sometimes you simply have to push yourself to go out."

From the house's patio, there is direct access to the office on the ground floor. With its own door, toilet and kitchen facility, the ground floor can function independently of the rest of the house.

The Gaaga office, located on the ground floor of the partners' residence. It is a basic space with large white tables and black office chairs. An oak floor adds a warm touch.

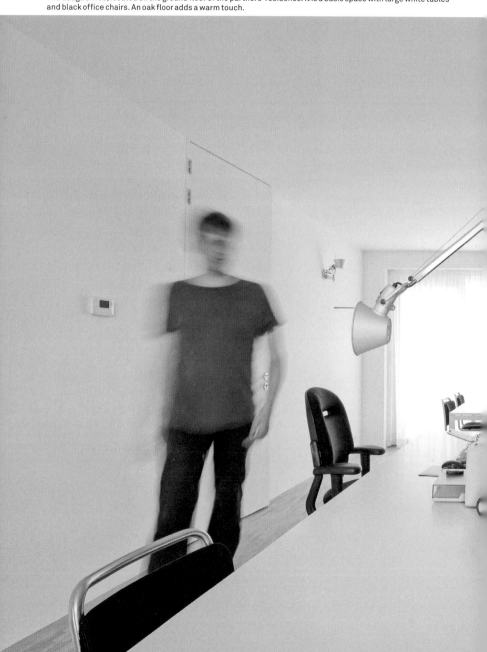

Louise Elling's chicken break: coffee and a newspaper for her, cheese crumbs for the chickens. It is part of the countryside idyll that she was looking for when she moved away from Copenhagen.

LOUISE SCHEELE ELLING, REMMARLÖV

User: Louise Scheele Elling
Industry: finance
Design: Louise Scheele Elling + Johan Lindell (renovation)
Location: Remmarlöv, Sweden
Size: 250 sq.m. / 2,690 sq.ft.
Completion: 2013 (original building 1850)

Her closest colleagues are chickens. That is what the Danish investor Louise Scheele Elling jokingly writes in a LinkedIn post about her work life in the Swedish countryside. Almost ten years ago, Louise and her Swedish husband Johan moved from a small apartment in Copenhagen to a spacious house in a village in Skåne, the southernmost county of Sweden. The village consists of only a few houses and a church, situated in a landscape of rolling farmland and small patches of forest. Louise's house is the village's old school. The building originates from 1850 and has been lovingly restored. It is filled with art, vintage furniture and all sorts of knick-knacks that the family has collected over the years. In the garden, there are fruit trees, a trampoline for the children, and, indeed, chickens.

In this pastoral setting, Louise runs a small investment company with stakes in real estate, a couple of start-up companies and various social projects. Louise explains: "I guess I could call myself an angel investor, but that would be too big a word. My main investments are time and energy, helping people to shape their ideas, coaching them, finding more partners and organizing funding—all with the intention of making good ideas come true and hopefully making a positive contribution to society."

Louise and her husband moved to the Swedish countryside because they were seeking more economic freedom and a better quality of life. "Compared to Copenhagen, living in the Swedish countryside is very cheap. Moreover, we wanted to have kids and the Swedish child care system is probably the best in the world. Our life here would not have been possible in Copenhagen. We have more space, more financial possibilities and more family time." And the countryside itself was another important reason for moving. "It may sound very hippie-like, but we wanted to be closer to nature."

The downside of this picture-perfect idyll is its remoteness. Louise's friends and the people she works with are relatively far away. Meeting places, such as cafés, clubs and galleries, are non-existent. Louise admits that maintaining her network would probably have been easier if she had still lived in Copenhagen, but she does not consider it a major problem. "Possibly I have a smaller network now, but it is more tight." Besides, her isolation is not as bad as it seems: "At least once a week I am in Malmö, Lund or Copenhagen for meetings, and my meetings are much more targeted than before. I've also made a habit of asking people over for lunch, which is very productive. Business becomes much more personal." In addition to these face-face contacts, Louise makes active use of social media, especially LinkedIn and Facebook, to remain visible and stay in touch with her network.

In order to be productive when working on your own, discipline is critical says Louise: "It is all too easy to fall into the trap of becoming some sort of housewife, wasting your working hours on laundry, dishes or vacuum cleaning." To avoid such domestic distractions, Louise adheres to strict working hours. Her days start with taking her children to school. On the way back in the car, she makes her first phone calls. At home, she settles in front of her laptop, writing emails, working on new ideas, checking up on her projects. At 10:30 she allows herself a 'chicken break', during which she feeds her chickens. Laughing, she says: "Chickens make great colleagues. They are good at listening and agree with everything I say. Everybody should have a chicken break." The end of her work day depends on whether it is her or her husband's turn to pick up the children. In either case, she stops working the moment the children are home, closing all her devices. "I quickly learned that I don't get anything done when the kids are there. I don't want be some sort of stressed mum, who gets irritated when the kids ask for attention. Being able to spend time with them was one of the reasons why we moved here."

When Louise is on the phone, she prefers to walk around as it avoids prolonged sitting at her small desk. It is also something of a necessity, because the building's solid walls block her mobile phone signal.

Louise has a small desk, located in a small corner of the television room. She has a more spacious workspace in the attic, but she prefers to be on the ground floor. Being distracted by her children is not an issue because she stops working as soon as they are home from school.

Type 2:
PUBLIC
SPACES

Work is ubiquitous. Using tablets, laptops and smartphones, people are tapping and talking in cafés, streets, parks, plazas and other public spaces. Working in public spaces is not always practical or comfortable, but it represents a certain degree of freedom and anonymity, being away from the confines of one's home or office. Another benefit of working 'out there' is the exposure to new activities, people and settings, which may spur creative thinking and lead to new contacts.

Their numbers may have dwindled, but on the streets of India one can still find so-called street typists. These 'typists-for-hire' fill in forms and write letters for people who are illiterate or lack the equipment or expertise to type up the papers they need. Simply by placing a stool and a small table on the pavement, street typists turn a piece of public space into an office, typically equipped with an old fashioned typewriter and sometimes even a Xerox machine to generate some extra turnover. In recent years, the presence of typists on India's streets has declined rapidly as literacy levels have risen and many Indians have acquired access to computers. However, the idea of using the street as an office is unlikely to disappear—quite the contrary, in fact. All over the world, pavements and plazas are populated by people who are texting and typing on mobile devices. Park benches and café tables are being appropriated as makeshift workplaces. Distracted walkers, engrossed in their smart phones, have become a common urban menace.[23] Some of these 'digital nomads' are merely updating their Facebook page or sending text messages to their friends, but many are also doing work-related activities, such as checking their email or sifting through cloud-stored files. They are the street typists of the 21st century.

Street typist in Kolkata, 2006. 'Typists-for-hire' are a dying profession as more and more people are literate and have access to computers. Even so, India's street typist remains a picturesque example of how outdoor spaces can be used as offices.

Working in public space is fundamentally different from working in an office. Inside an office, people are surrounded by colleagues who share the same organizational context: they know each other, have the same boss, sit at identical desks, eat the same food in the same canteen, follow a similar dress code, et cetera. In that sense, office buildings are rather homogeneous, inward-oriented and predictable work environments. They are places that are shielded from the outside world by sealed facades, biometric access systems, card readers, and security staff whose sole objective is to keep alien and unwanted elements outside. In contrast, public spaces offer an open, exposed and unpredictable work environment. Working there means working amid strangers. Unexpected events and encounters can occur, which may be either stimulating and inspirational, or disturbing and annoying. One practical difference between offices and public spaces is that the latter are generally not designed for work. Although more and more public spaces provide Wi-Fi, power outlets and comfortable seating, working on a park bench or wobbly café chair is still very different from sitting on an ergonomic office chair in an air-conditioned office. It is not only a matter of ergonomics, but also of sounds and activities. In public

Modern street typist in London, 2011. This city worker is seated on a concrete bench with his laptop, enjoying the early spring sunshine.

spaces, distraction comes not from chatting colleagues, but from the noise of passers-by and traffic, or possibly just from chirping birds and rustling leaves. Furthermore, public spaces tend to lack specific office facilities such as printers, large computer screens and secured networks. All this can make working in public space rather impractical if done for extended periods of time.

Even so, the American designer Jonathan Olivares sees public spaces as untapped potential. Olivares has made an extensive study of open-air workplaces, titled *The Outdoor Office*.[24] Olivares sees outdoor workspaces as a natural and healthy extension of the indoor environment. In addition, working outdoors can be seen as a sustainable solution. The use of materials is low and energy-consuming technical systems, such office lighting and HVAC systems, are absent. As part of the project, Olivares came up with a number of design proposals for outdoor work settings. Using UV-resistant shields, these proposals solve practical issues such as glare from direct sunlight or the risk of wind blowing one's papers away. Olivares' designs would probably prove quite popular in public places that are frequented by business people and students, such as New York's Bryant Park (see page 53). It is also

Hypothetical design of an outdoor workspace, part of the 'The Outdoor Office' project by Jonathan Olivares. A canvas screen provides an individual worker with shelter from sun and wind.

clear, however, that some inherent problems of outdoor working will always remain. Depending on location and the time of year, these can be heat, cold and humidity or other natural irritants such as flies and mosquitoes.

Indoor public spaces can be more comfortable alternatives. Walk into any coffee place in any large city, and you are likely to find people staring at glowing screens (unless it is one of the few cafés that has adopted a 'no laptop' policy). Typical 'coffice' workers are mobile business people in need of a temporary workplace, freelancers who want to get out of the house, and students who find the library too quiet. The practice is so popular that there is an app called 'Worksnug' that helps people to find coffee bars and other public spaces that are suitable for work. The app indicates the noise level, the availability of power and Wi-Fi, and the 'vibe' of the place—thereby neatly summing up the main concerns of the modern-day mobile worker looking for a place to work.

The current popularity of using cafés as workplaces is closely related to emergence of Wi-Fi and mobile computing in the 1990s, but it is actually an age-old practice that can be traced back to the 17th century, when London's first coffee houses were established. These were venues

Cartoon of Lloyd's Coffee House in London by George Woodward, 1798. London's early coffee houses were popular places for doing business—long before the emergence Wi-Fi and caffè lattes.

where people could drink coffee and read newspapers, but they were also places for trade, dealmaking and information gathering. The most famous example is Lloyd's Coffee House, which was a meeting place for merchants, shipowners, sailors and insurance brokers. At the coffee house, they could acquire maritime information and arrange insurance for cargos and ships. Later, Lloyd's Coffee House would evolve into the Lloyd's insurance market, which now occupies one of London's most striking office buildings.

Cafés have also always been popular places to work for writers and poets. In his biography, the American writer Ernest Hemingway explained how, in winter, he would escape the cold of his Parisian apartment and go to a café where he would "work all morning over a café crème while the waiters cleaned and swept out the café and it gradually grew warmer."[25] A contemporary example is J.K. Rowling who famously worked on her first Harry Potter novel in the back room of an Edinburgh café called The Elephant House—which now has a sign on its facade declaring it 'The Birthplace of Harry Potter'.

Despite their bohemian appeal, cafés have their disadvantages as places for work. They can pose practical challenges (i.e. what to do with

Café in London, 2012. Today's cafés are once again popular places for office work. A notable difference with London's 17th-century coffee houses is that contemporary café workers are quiet, focused on their laptop screens rather than interacting with the clientele.

one's laptop during a toilet break?) and they can be noisy and crowded, depending on the type of locale. A quiet alternative is the library: also a public venue, but with the benefit of actually being designed for knowledge work. Libraries offer the unique quality of silence combined with an atmosphere of scholarship. Reading rooms are populated by people with laptops, working on their own in the hushed presence of others—which may add a welcome kind of peer pressure to be productive. According to a 2013 survey by the US Information Policy and Access Center, more than half of the American public libraries offer workspace for mobile workers.[26]

In travel-related public places, such as airports and aeroplanes, hotel lobbies and train stations, working is often just a constructive way of 'killing' time. These are spaces where people are essentially captive and work helps make travel hours more productive. Some people even deliberately seek out such spaces as a spur to productivity. James Attlee, an English writer, said of working in trains: "The train gave me the space and the externally imposed routine to complete three books. I imagined that when I stopped commuting and had more time at home my productivity as a writer would increase exponentially. The reverse

Man working on a train in Germany, 2009. Many trains now offer Wi-Fi and power outlets to allow travellers to make efficient use of their time. Travel hours become working hours.

was true. It seems that rather than needing solitude, I am a man of the crowd who thinks best while moving at speed between two points, neither here nor there."[27]
Attlee's comment points to an interesting quality of public space, which is that they are 'in-between spaces'. They are neither office nor home. People are surrounded by strangers rather than co-workers or family members. Because of that, public spaces provide a certain privacy and anonymity, and thereby a sense of freedom. Obviously there are distractions in public spaces, such as loud people or pushy waiters, but they are of a different category than colleagues or family members demanding serious attention.

There are critics who argue that the use of laptops, phones and other digital devices erodes the social life of public spaces. Their concern is that many people, and certainly mobile workers, are only 'absently present' in public space: physically there, but more absorbed in their mobile devices than engaged with their direct surroundings. [28] Evidence for this comes from an observational study by Tali Hatuka and Eran Toch from the University of Tel Aviv, which shows that smartphone users tend to be more detached from their physical surroundings than those who use traditional phones (i.e. phones without Internet access).[29] According to the researchers, smartphone users give the impression of moving through communal spaces as if in private bubbles or "portable private personal territories", which coincides neatly with Hans Hollein's early idea of the mobile office as a see-through plastic bubble, see page 7.
To what extent the use of technology really will have a negative impact on the social life of public spaces remains to be seen. There are also studies that suggest that public spaces will be used by more people and more intensely, as people will use public space for activities which people would otherwise have performed in the office or at home.[30] Either way, public spaces are an interesting supplement to the more insular way of working in office buildings. The virtue of public spaces is that they provide exposure to a diversity of people, activities and settings that cannot be found, or mimicked, in an office—no matter how hard architects these days try to design offices as metaphorical cities. This exposure can be bothersome, but it may also be beneficial to people's work. A walk in the park may help to clear a mental block. Working in a library may stimulate one's scholarly zeal. Overhearing a conversation on the train may trigger new thoughts. A chance encounter in a café may

be the start of a new venture. Being 'out there' may also give people a sense of energy and dynamism, of being part of something bigger than just their work or family. It may even remind today's busy street typists that there is more to life than work.

Visitor sitting on Bryant Park's Great Lawn, making use of the park's free Wi-Fi, while seated (somewhat uncomfortably?) on the grass.

BRYANT PARK, NEW YORK

Users: various
Industry: various
Design: Hanna/Olin and Lynden B. Miller
Location: New York, United States
Size: 39,000 sq.m. / 9,603 acre
Completion: 1992 (re-design/renovation) / 2002 (Wi-Fi installed)

Bryant Park was the first of New York's parks to provide free Wi-Fi to its users. Ever since, the park has been a popular work spot. Especially on sunny days, the park is filled with people doing work-like activities. Beneath the trees and in the meadows, people are typing on laptops, reading on e-readers and swiping tablet screens. Men in suits stroll on the park's gravel paths, making phone calls or sending text messages from their smartphones. On such days, Bryant Park is a true office landscape.

One of the park's frequent users is Craig Nelson, a freelance writer and editor living in New York. Craig works from home, but also in cafés, libraries and public spaces like Bryant Park. He explains: "I come here about once a week during summer, spring and fall. I tend to use it in the early afternoon when I need some fresh air after being in the nearby New York Public Library all morning." To Craig, the great benefit of working in the park lies in the atmosphere. "Being surrounded by greenery and the sounds of the city is inspiring to me. When I don't need silence, the hum of New York is a great backdrop for doing work."

The Bryant Park set-up facilitates the activities of people like Craig. There are tables and chairs scattered throughout the park. Large trees provide plenty of shade. Coffee can be bought from the park's kiosks. There is Wi-Fi and recently power outlets were added as well. Bryant Park's website trumpets: "Go wireless and turn Bryant Park into your new office. Your clients will be impressed with your front lobby."

The park has not always been so successful. In the 1970s it was notorious for drug dealing and prostitution. To counter the decline, the park was radically redesigned in the late 1980s. Much of the makeover was based on the work of the highly respected American urbanist William Whyte. The park's original shrubberies and iron fences were removed to improve visual overview and make it more accessible. Kiosks, public restrooms and an entertainment programme were added. A typical William Whyte intervention was the addition of movable chairs. In his classic book *The Social Life of Small Urban Spaces*, Whyte wrote: "Chairs enlarge choice: to move into the sun, out of it, to make room for groups, to move away from them. The possibility of choice is as important as the exercise of it. If you know you can move if you want to, you feel more comfortable staying put."[31]

It is impossible to know what William Whyte would have thought of the provision of Wi-Fi in Bryant Park. It could be argued that Wi-Fi has a negative impact on the social life of public spaces because people are staring at their screens rather than taking part in what is happening around them. Another interpretation, however, is that Wi-Fi is bringing new activities to public spaces, attracting more people, and causing them to stay longer than before.

For Craig Nelson, the availability of Wi-Fi is one of the reasons why he spends time in Bryant Park. It allows him to use the park as an informal workplace, although he does not do all his work there. "I usually catch up with emails and do some of my more routine work or brainstorming." For more demanding tasks, he considers the park less suitable: "Sometimes there is too much activity that can distract me from working. Also, quite a number of people will come up and ask for change, or just interrupt your flow of work. That can make it hard to concentrate for long periods of time." But this does not dampen his enthusiasm for Bryant Park. "If you can find a piece of shade on a beautiful day, it's hard to beat this as a unique NYC office space."

Laptop worker in Bryant Park, apparently not much hindered by glare on her computer screen.

On sunny days, Bryant Park in New York is crowded with people. Real estate figures show that the rental levels of the office buildings around the park outperform the rest of New York's Midtown.[32]

Woman staring at her computer screen at the Coffee Company in Rotterdam. There is Wi-Fi, power, coffee and a horizontal work surface for a laptop—all the basic requirements for office work.

COFFEE COMPANY, ROTTERDAM

Users: self-employed workers, business people, students
Industry: various
Design: Concern
Location: Rotterdam, the Netherlands
Size: 90 sq.m./ 969 sq.ft.
Completion: 2011

On a rainy Tuesday morning, it is quiet at the Coffee Company in Rotterdam. But those who are there do seem to be quite productive. Two consultants are sitting at the large reading table, chatting in front of an open laptop. They explain that they are having a 'pre-meeting' before they go to visit a client. A lone, suited businessman is seated at one of the café tables, tapping on his smartphone. A female student sits at the bar table in the window bay, sipping a large hot chocolate and staring at her iBook screen.

It is a normal scene at the Coffee Company. This Dutch chain of coffee bars is popular among self-employed professionals, business people, and students who use it as an alternative to their home, office or the library. A few years ago, the use of cafés for such purposes was a topic of debate in the Netherlands, as in many other places. In the media, there were stories about cafés adopting no-laptop policies. The argument was that 'laptop loafers' and 'Wi-Fi squatters' were occupying seats for extended periods while spending relatively little. Another argument was that this type of clientele add little to the café atmosphere as they tend to be immersed in what is happening on their screens. These days, however, the use of laptops and other electronic devices has become commonplace in cafés—and virtually everywhere.

At the Coffee Company, they consider laptop users an important part of their client base and deliberately cater to their needs. Openings hours are early. Power outlets can be found under tables, in benches and underneath the bar. Wi-Fi is almost free: the login name and password are printed on the receipt and valid for an hour. The barista of the Coffee Company in Rotterdam explains: "If you want more, just order another drink or snack."

Gilian Schrofer is co-founder and creative director of the Dutch design firm Concern, which designed the first generation of Coffee Company outlets as well as some more recent ones, including the one in Rotterdam. He explains: "In the design of the Coffee Company's cafés, work activities are explicitly taken into account. The large reading table, for example, has become a defining feature. It's popular among laptop users because it offers a large horizontal work surface and power sockets. In addition, we look at things like lighting levels, seating heights and the spatial zoning of the café."

The interior design of the Coffee Company in Rotterdam is basic, hip and cosy, with whitewashed walls, a wooden floor, a tiled counter and vintage furniture. To accommodate the needs of different types of customers, there are different types of seating. Low benches and leather sofas for lounging. Bistro tables for small groups. A large reading table and a bar-style table for people with laptops and others who prefer to sit by themselves.

Gilian Schrofer explains that his firm uses its experience with café design for the design of office environments. "If you look at our office projects, you will notice lots of social areas that look very café-like, with casual design, benches, booths, counters and professional espresso machines. That is quite deliberate. In offices, pantries and canteens are no longer just functional facilities for coffee or lunch, but also places to hang out and meet others. They facilitate a more informal type of interaction, which is seen as critical for knowledge sharing in organizations."

At the Coffee Company in Rotterdam, however, there is not much interaction going on this Tuesday morning. It may be too early and, unlike in a regular office, people don't know one other. The customers are focused on their devices. Access to Wi-Fi and caffeine seem sufficient for them to be productive. Their only practical consideration may be the use of the toilet facilities, which are two stairs up. What to do with one's laptop during a toilet break? Familiar with the issue, the barista says he would be happy to keep an eye on it.

Woman reading a newspaper at the Coffee Company in Rotterdam—one of the few people not using an electronic device.

Two men working together at the Coffee Company in Rotterdam, probably preparing for a meeting or presentation. The receipts for their drinks lie besides their computers. Printed on the receipts are the login details for an hour's access to the wireless network.

Guests and visitors working in leather chesterfields in the lobby of the Ace Hotel in New York. From the bar next to them, they can order coffee, drinks and snacks.

ACE HOTEL, NEW YORK

User: business travellers, tourists, nomadic workers
Industry: mostly creative sector
Design: Roman and Williams
Location: New York, United States
Size: 16,630 sq.m. / 179,000 sq.ft. (total hotel)
Completion: 2009

Hotel lobbies are often little more than circulation areas. There are people arriving and leaving. Checking in and out. Waiting for friends or taxis. Some lobbies, however, are destinations in themselves. The lobby of the Ace Hotel in New York is a renowned example. The hotel is housed in a historic, turn-of-the-century building. It has a vast, monumental lobby, which is usually a hive of activity. There are people hanging out, drinking coffee, reading newspapers and talking to friends. Alongside these more leisurely activities, many people are working: checking their emails, writing, preparing presentations or conducting business meetings. It is a mix of relaxation, work and networking that is taking place here.

Interestingly, the Ace Hotel lobby is used not only by hotel guests, but also by local New Yorkers. After its opening in 2009, the hotel quickly acquired a reputation as a gathering place for members of New York's creative class. Designers, writers, advertising people, fashion figures and other hip professionals started to use the hotel as a meeting spot and workplace.

The Ace Hotel's management is quite happy to have these 'non-guests' in their lobby. An Ace representative says: "We have always envisioned our hotel as a hub of creative energy in the neighbourhood. The lobby is a public space, and we find that guests mingle with the public in the lobby to much success. By creating on open space for all, there's an air of collaboration and friendliness in the lobby that benefits everyone."

The success of the Ace lobby can be attributed to a number of different factors. At a basic level there are the free Wi-Fi, the power outlets and the availability of good coffee (from the lobby-side Stumptown coffee shop). Just as important is the unobtrusive staff who provide service, but not so much as to make people feel uncomfortable.

An important spatial quality is the size of the lobby. It is much larger than the lobbies of other, more economically designed hotels, providing more seating and many different kinds of seating. The most popular work spot is an old laboratory table that stands in the middle of the lobby. It is a long table with a slate top and vintage brass desk lamps, large enough to accommodate ten people with laptops, papers and cups of coffee. In addition, there are English wing chairs, leather chesterfields and 1970s-style suede couches one can sink into with a laptop or iPad on one's knees.

Last but not least, is the ambience. The lobby is an impressive space, with coffered ceilings, plaster mouldings, classical columns and a mosaic floor. The design firm Roman and Williams decorated this space with an eclectic mix of furniture from different eras, contemporary art and 'found objects' such as apothecary cabinets, old school chairs and a French bakery table. This 'shabby chic' decor is not for everybody, but it seems fitting for the fashionable and hip crowd that frequents the hotel. The bohemian atmosphere probably makes working there a more special experience than working at home or in the office. On the Foursquare social network, a hotel visitor notes that the live music jams that take place in the lobby and the rustic lighting will "make you feel cool typing on your MacBook". [33]

A practical advantage of working in a hotel lobby is that it is always open. Traditional office hours do not apply here. A potential disadvantage is that the lobby can be crowded. Despite its spaciousness, it may be difficult to find a seat, especially at weekends and in the evenings. There are people having drinks at the bar and in the evenings there is a DJ playing music. So, conditions may not always be favourable for work activities. Even so, the Ace Hotel aims for a happy coexistence of all types of activities in its lobby, work and non-work. The Ace representative says: "Everyone doing their own thing allows the space to be brimming with possibility, and having that energy around is really positive."

Part of the popularity of the Ace Hotel's lobby as a place of work lies in the staff, who are unobtrusive: providing service without being too 'pushy', which would probably make non-guests feel uncomfortable.

The large table in the centre of the Ace Hotel's lobby is never empty. Both guests and non-guests like to work there. Note the vintage brass desk lamps and the mosaic floor, which add to the bohemian atmosphere in the lobby.

Type 3:

CO-WORK OFFICES

Co-work offices are workspaces where you can rent desks on a monthly or daily basis, but the concept is about more than just desks. The central idea is that people share office facilities along with a sense of community, allowing for collaboration, networking and synergies. Co-workspaces are mostly popular among freelancers and independent workers, many of them in the creative sector. That makes it a bit of a 'hipster' phenomenon, but the concept is rapidly becoming more mainstream, with the corporate world also taking an interest.

In 2005, the American software programmer Brad Neuberg quit his job at a large corporation and started to work as a freelancer. While happy with his escape from the corporate world, he missed the company of others and the structure of working in an office.[34] This prompted him to start the 'Spiral Muse co-working community', which consisted of eight desks, a couple of sofas and a kitchenette in a women's centre in San Francisco. The desks could be hired for a hundred dollars a month. As the promotional website put it: "Do you work for yourself from home? Do you miss community and structure? Join Spiral Muse and Brad Neuberg in creating a new kind of work environment for free spirits!"[35]

Neuberg envisioned that he and the other free spirits would act as a collective, sharing not only space, but also a particular mode of work. He proposed that they would start the day with a short meditation session ("to check in physically and emotionally where we are"[36]) and that there would be a midday break for a group activity like yoga, a walk or a bike ride. Working days would end at 5:45 PM sharp ("ending our work in a healthy, balanced way"[37]).

Neuberg's initiative entered workplace history as the first formal co-workspace. This is not entirely accurate because similar concepts had

Brad Neuberg and another co-worker at the Spiral Muse Co-working Community, 1995, the first co-workspace to style itself as such. The promotional website appealed to readers thus: "Tired of working from coffee shops every day? Miss community and structure in your work life? Try Co-working!"[47]

emerged elsewhere as well (e.g. Republikken in Copenhagen, see p. 87), but these did not use the term co-working. The concept, too, had several precedents. In the 1980s, so-called 'office hotels' and 'executive suites' had emerged where business people could rent space on a membership basis. Co-work purists point out, however, that these commercial concepts lacked the sense of community that is at the heart of co-working. Also similar in many ways to co-working are the 'telework centres' and 'neighbourhood work centres' of the 1990s. They were conceived as shared office spaces for telecommuters, located close to their homes to reduce commuting time, and intended to be used by people from different organizations.[38]

Going even further back in history, co-working may be seen as a contemporary interpretation of the age-old practice of artists or writers teaming up to rent studio space, sharing space and each other's company.[39] It even brings to mind 19th-century English gentlemen's clubs, which operated on a membership basis and were productive places for building networks and exchanging business information.[40] Notwithstanding all these historical precedents, co-working is clearly a very contemporary phenomenon that is closely connected to the

Drawing of a gentlemen's club in London, by D.T. Egerton, 1824. These clubs can be seen as co-work offices avant la lettre. They were membership-based places where people came to socialize, build networks and exchange information.

21st-century 'flexibilization' of labour. Up until the late 1980s, most office workers were employed in large organizations, with full-time, long-term labour contracts. In recent decades there has been a radical shift towards more self-employment, part-time work and widespread freelancing. This has in turn created a large pool of 'footloose' professionals who are in need of a flexible place to work.

For many of these professionals, working from home is the most obvious choice because it is cheap and flexible. But as Brad Neuberg experienced, working from home can be lonely. An alternative is to work in public spaces, like cafés or libraries (see chapter 2), or to rent a room in a serviced office. These options, however, can be either impractical or pricey. Co-working is interesting because it tries to combine the advantages of all these options: the low costs and flexibility of working at home, the social life of a café, and the professional facilities of a serviced office.

In this mix, the social aspect is regarded as the most defining. Wikipedia explicitly describes co-working as the gathering of a group of people "who share values, and who are interested in the synergy that can happen from working with talented people in the same space."[41] In line

Outdoor sign of TheOffice, a co-workspace in Santa Monica. The sign explains the advantages of co-working, targeting those who are tired of working in coffee bars or who find working from home too stressful (Photo: Niall Kennedy / Flickr)

with the emphasis on sharing values, co-working is often presented under the idealistic banner of the 'shared economy', which stresses the importance of the shared use of resources for the sake not only of sustainability, but also of community building.[42]

At the moment, there are estimated to be about 2,500 co-workspaces across the world, with a total of about 110,000 active members.[43] Large cities, such Berlin, London and New York, have over 60 co-workspaces each. These figures are impressive for such a young phenomenon, but obviously it is still rather marginal when compared with the large numbers of conventional office buildings and the vast numbers of ordinary 'salary men' who work in them.

A 2010 survey conducted by the co-working journal *Deskmag* found that co-working is still a bit of hipster phenomenon. The overwhelming majority of co-workers are active in the creative industries and in new media.[44] Many of them are web developers, programmers, graphic designers, journalists, writers, architects and artists, and all sorts of coaches and consultants. Most of them are in their mid-twenties to late thirties. In terms of fashion stereotypes it is skinny jeans and designer glasses rather than suits and ties.

In coming years, however, the concept is likely to become more mainstream. As economic difficulties persist and corporations continue to 'downsize' their organizations, more people will be pushed into starting up their own business. In addition, growth will come from employed professionals who make their own, deliberate choice to escape the corporate world and seek more autonomy and flexibility. New generations of workers will enter the workforce, who seem more willing than earlier generations to start their own business and work for themselves, choosing freedom over security.[45] All this may increase the demand for cheap, flexible and social office space.

Furthermore, large corporations have started to take an interest in the co-working concept. Perhaps unsurprisingly, the tech giant Google has taken the lead in this development. In London, Google has created its own large co-work venue, called Campus. This seven-storey building offers cheap space, free events and mentoring for start-ups and tech entrepreneurs. Registered users can use the café area for free and there are rentable desks for start-ups. Google refers to it as an 'open source building',[46] and only uses the top floor for its own staff.

For Google, creating its own co-workspace may be very advantageous because it provides them with an entry point into London's dense networks of tech talents and promising start-ups. Similar motives apply to companies like HP, Cisco and Zappos, who are experimenting with co-work facilities inside their offices. For other organizations, co-working may be mostly of practical benefit. Companies without an extensive office network can use co-workspaces to facilitate travelling staff or people who live a long way from a corporate office. Many co-workspaces offer corporate memberships to attract these kinds of users. New initiatives like 'Copass' allow people to gain access to co-workspaces across the world. Furthermore, there are web-based tools such as 'LiquidSpace' that help people to find co-workspaces and meeting rooms for just a day or an hour in any city, checking real-time availability and pricing.

When co-working is considered in the wider discussion about the future of the office, it is interesting to observe that despite all the revolutionary rhetoric and their cool design, co-workspaces are still essentially offices: spaces with desks where people go to work and have meetings with others. Just as with conventional offices, the basic assumption is that people are more productive when they are physically

StartUp Weekend at Google's co-workspace in London. Google Campus offers free events, rentable desks for start-ups and free workspace in the building's café for registered users. (Photo: Bayerberg / Flickr)

together in a space that is purpose-designed for work. The essential difference lies in the sourcing model: conventional office workers go to the office because they have to, no matter the quality of the coffee or the noisiness of the workspace. In contrast, co-workers go to the office of their own free will, and if they are not happy with the quality of the offering, they simply go somewhere else.

The 'focus area' in Impact Hub Amsterdam. It is the part of the office where people can work in relative peace and quiet during the day. In the evenings and at weekends the space is often transformed into an event space for performances, exhibitions and parties.

IMPACT HUB, AMSTERDAM

Users: social entrepreneurs
Industry: various
Design: AKKA
Location: Amsterdam, The Netherlands
Size: 600 sq.m./ 6,458 sq.ft.
Completion: 2013

The Impact Hub in Amsterdam is a place for idealists. It is a co-workspace that is specifically targeted at social entrepreneurs. That is a broad category but in this case it means people working in fields such as sustainability, corporate social responsibility, human rights and personal development. There are designers, product developers, all sorts of consultants and quite a number of coaches. Most of them are self-employed and independent.

Milena Kriek is manager of the Impact Hub in Amsterdam. She explains: "Our members aim to have a positive impact on society, hence the name Impact Hub." The prime purpose of the Impact Hub is to help its members in achieving this. Milena: "We believe that impact cannot happen in isolation, it requires collective action. At the Impact Hub, our members can access the resources, knowledge and talent to move their initiatives for a better world forward." To facilitate their members, the Impact Hub offers workspace, but also mentoring and training programmes for entrepreneurs in all stages of development and, probably most important of all, access to a community of like-minded people.

The Impact Hub in Amsterdam is not an isolated upsurge of idealism, but part of a wide network of Impact Hubs across the world. The first Impact Hub (originally just called 'The Hub') was established in London in 2005. Since then, the Impact Hub has grown into an international association with more than fifty locations on six continents, and over seven thousand members.

The Impact Hub in Amsterdam is located on the site of the Westergasfabriek—a redeveloped gas factory on the edge of Amsterdam's city centre. It is a vibrant area, home to creative companies, cultural institutions, restaurants and cafés. The Impact

Hub occupies the first floor of the factory's former administration building. It is an elegant red brick building that dates from the end of the 19th century. Inside, spaces are large and filled with light. Tall windows provide a view of the surrounding park. Much of the furniture is second-hand or self-made. Desks are made of recycled cardboard and placed on wheels so they can easily be pushed aside to make room for the events that take place in the evenings and at weekends.

There are two main work areas at the Impact Hub: a 'focus area' and a 'café area'. The focus area provides a studious atmosphere. People work there quietly, concentrating on their computer screens. In contrast, the 'café area' is more lively, with the sounds of chatter, background music and the grinding of the coffee machine.

The Impact Hub offers about 100 workplaces for over 300 members. This ratio works because there are different types of memberships. The majority of members have a 'limited', flexible membership that allows them to use unassigned desks for a numbers of days a week. A limited number of people have a 'team desk' membership that gives them 24/7 access, plus an assigned desk and personal storage.

Small companies have the possibility to rent one of the three enclosed office spaces in the building. This is a new feature, as Milena explains: "Originally, we only provided desks for individuals. Some of our members, however, have grown from individual entrepreneurs into small companies with staff. Previously this meant that they had to move out. Now companies can grow and remain part of our community."

The Impact Hub's spaces can also be rented by non-members for meetings, workshops and events. This has proven to be popular. Milena: "There are many organizations that want to hold events and meetings here. They come to experience something different, away from their usual work environment, and to absorb some of the vibe and energy of the Impact Hub."

Renting out space is an important source of revenue for the Impact Hub, but Milena insists that it is not their core business: "We are not a serviced office. Our main offering is our community of impact-makers, working together to build a more sustainable world. We want to be a place where people can tap into a wealth of experience, get inspiration and meet new people who can help them further. Rather than just a workspace, we are an ecosystem for change."

Leaf-shaped desks in the Impact Hub's café area. The desks allow for high-density working and are made from recycled cardboard, which is in line with the Impact Hub's sustainability ambitions.

Café area in the Impact Hub. Note the banner: "Impact cannot happen in isolation. It requires collective action." The idea of the Impact Hub is that sharing workspace helps to spur such collective action.

Workshop space at Republikken. Republikken offers much more than just desk space. Given that it is targeted at creative professionals, it also provides access to professional tools such as a laser cutter, vinyl plotter and 3D printer.

REPUBLIKKEN, COPENHAGEN

Users: freelancers, self-employed professionals
Industry: creative sector (design/graphics/text)
Design: Republikken
Location: Copenhagen (Denmark)
Size: 2000 sq.m./ 21,528 sq.ft.
Year: 2005, later additions: 2012-2013

The Danish co-workspace Republikken was one the first co-workspaces in Europe, although they actually do not use the term co-working. Instead, they call themselves an 'arbejdsfællesskab', which can best be translated as a 'work community'. Republikken was started in 2005 by a group of friends who wanted to have a space to work. Gradually, the initiative became an important nucleus of Copenhagen's creative scene. There are now over 100 members. It is a hip, casually dressed crowd—mostly freelancers and independent professionals, working in the fields of design, graphics, photography, illustration, architecture and communication.

The co-workspace is located in a turn-of-the-century building in Copenhagen's gritty yet trendy Vesterbro area. Inside, the building provides the kind of raw and cool look one expects of a creative hotspot, with high ceilings, wooden floors and whitewashed walls. There are vintage lamps and sofas, self-made wooden desks and various art objects created by Republikken's members.

Ivan Lopez Garrido is Republikken's 'office captain', who makes sure that the co-workspace functions as it should, taking care of practicalities, answering questions, helping new members to integrate, and organizing communal activities. Ivan explains that most of Republikken's members are experienced professionals in their thirties or older. "They are not youngsters just out of education, but people who have already worked for some years and made a deliberate choice to work on their own rather than being employed in a large company." There is also a two-person company, with its own separate space, but they are an exception. Ivan explains: "There is no rule that you have to move out if you start a firm with others, but that is how it goes. Small firms tend to want a space of their own." The workstations at Republikken are divided over three separate areas, each of them occupied by a different, loosely defined group: 'text people' (e.g. journalists), 'visuals' (e.g. illustrators) and designers (e.g. architects). At a certain point, there was a move to mix these disciplines to stimulate cross-fertilization, but it did not survive. Ivan explains: "Putting people from the same discipline together is practical because they have similar work patterns, face similar issues and they can help one another." And it is not as if these groups are closed communities. Members meet each other in the shared kitchenette, at communal lunches, at the Friday bars and at the parties that are frequently organized to strengthen the social ties between members.

At the moment, Republikken has 75 workstations and about 100 members. Some of the desks are unassigned, intended for flexible use, but most of Republikken's members rent a fixed desk which they use on a daily basis. Having a personal desk is considered practical by many members because they are working with specific devices such as drawing tablets and large computer screens that they do not want to carry around all the time. Some of the members have even bought their own ergonomic furniture. A practical advantage of having one's own desk, is that it is possible to personalize it. Officially, all desks should be clean, but that policy is not strictly enforced. Many of the desks are covered with creative artefacts such as sketch rolls, printouts, books, design magazines and 3D-printed objects. "We are not really into strict rules or policing here," notes Ivan.

In addition to the desk areas, Republikken provides professional workshop facilities. Members can make use of a 3D printer, a laser cutter and a vinyl plotter to make prototypes of their designs. There are various meetings rooms, which are often rented out to external parties. A 'Republikken school' was set up to provide courses in topics like graphic design and laser cutting, targeted at both members and non-members. Most recently, a café was added on the first floor, which is open the public and furnished with objects made by Republikken's own designers and architects.

With all these additional functions, Republikken is evolving into a place that is much more than just a co-work office with desks. It is an office-slash-workshop-slash-café-slash-school. With good reason, Republikken refers to itself as a 'platform' for freelancers and small businesses, aimed at providing everything that is needed to be a successful creative professional in Copenhagen.

Republikken's café is open to members and non-members. If you plan to work there for a full day, you are expected to buy a 'work pass' for about 50 DKK (6.70 EUR/9 USD), for which you get free tea and coffee, and a 10% discount on food, drinks and meeting rooms.

The work areas at Republikken are loosely organized around three creative disciplines: text, design and visuals. Each discipline has its own 'wing' to allow easy collaboration and learning. Interaction between the disciplines takes places in the central kitchenette and during the communal lunches and the Friday bar.

The main workspace at Mutinerie. There are no strict rules about making a noise, but generally people work quietly. Many wear headphones to listen to music or shut out the sounds of others.

MUTINERIE, PARIS

Users: freelancers, self-employed professionals
Industry: various
Design: Mutinerie and Marie Prenat
Location: Paris, France
Size: 400 sq.m./ 4,305 sq.ft.
Completion: 2010

Free Together. That is the motto of the Mutinerie, a co-workspace in Paris founded by Eric van den Broek together with his two brothers and a childhood friend. He explains: "We started this place because of our own needs. A couple of years ago, we decided we wanted to work as independents. We wanted to escape from traditional organizational structures. To rebel against corporate conventions. But we also wanted to work in a community, together with others."

Mutinerie started out small, but currently offers 70 workstations to around 160 members. The members are called 'Mutins', which is French for Mutineers. Among them are typical freelance professionals, such as consultants, bloggers and designers, but there are other types of users as well, including a lawyer, several students and—this being Paris— even a 'pâtissier' who uses the place to work on his business plan. Some of the members come on a daily basis, others once a week or less. The composition of the group is dynamic, and according to Eric that is how it should be: "If there were only regulars, it would dry up at a certain point. We want a steady flow of new people coming in, creating possibilities for new connections and the exchange of new ideas."

Eric notes that there is a certain challenge in making newcomers feel at home. "Entering a co-workspace for the first time can be a bit like one's first day at school. You're new and all the others seem to know one another. But, by the end of the day, you are likely to have had a chat with five, maybe six people, and then it starts to feel good. People go from shy to enthusiastic."

The Mutinerie space is designed in such a way that it promotes contact and inclusion. Eric says: "You cannot simply just tell people to collaborate and then expect it to happen. And we don't want to push people. So we have tried to create natural conditions for collaboration."

One of the things Eric and his colleagues did to promote interaction was to position the café area right behind the entrance. "So as people are coming in they are almost always passing others, which increases the chances for an informal chat or at least a greeting before starting to work at one's computer."

Another intervention was to make all desks shared. Eric: "In the beginning we had some fixed desks for regulars. We noticed, however, that when people have their own desk, they start to behave differently. They become more protective and seem more sensitive to distractions. So we decided that all workplaces would be shared. Everybody has the same rights here."

Mutinerie's main workspace is a big open space, with lots of plants, a variety of desks and a ping-pong table that is appropriated as a work table. There are people working concentratedly on their laptop computers, many of them wearing headphones. Some are chatting, but with lowered voices. Eric says: "We were surprised about the quietness. We actually don't have any rules on this. When we opened the space there was some clapping after the opening speech, and then people just started to work. It has been like that ever since." For noisy activities, members go to the café area. Phone calls can be taken in the enclosed phone booths. For those who need total quiet, there is a library-like space. Meetings can be held in the workshop spaces in the building's basement.

Now that Mutinerie is working as it should, Eric van den Broek has started a new project called Copass. Copass is a membership structure that gives people access to affiliated co-working spaces across the world. Eric: "It allows independents and small companies to work internationally, making use of an inexpensive global infrastructure." The project is still in its early stages, but is already attracting a lot of interest. The mutiny spreads.

Mutinerie's kitchenette and social area. The café-like area is positioned right at the entrance. Everybody has to pass through it when entering the space, increasing opportunities for conversations and encounters.

Work benches in Mutinerie's 'garage'. Traffic cones act as overhead lighting. These and other unconventional design solutions were developed by the Mutinerie members themselves, in collaboration with architect Marie Prenat.

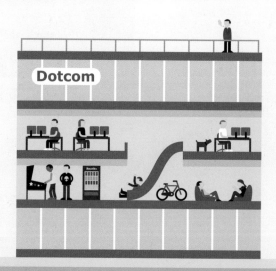

Type 4:
PLAY OFFICES

Some offices seem too good or too 'wacky' to be true: offices with slides, miniature golf courses and pop-art style design. Tech companies such as Google and Facebook are famous for such 'play offices'. Their cheerful work environments are testament to the importance of attracting and retaining young talent in the highly competitive Internet business. They are also an expression of a 'work hard, play hard' ethic where leisurely activities go hand-in-hand with long hours and a frantic work pace.

On the Internet, you can find lists on almost any topic, including workplace design. Typical list titles are 'the world's ten most awesome workplaces' or 'ten outrageously cool office interiors'. Invariably, these lists are headed by eye-catching offices with playful features such as basketball hoops or skate ramps. Such 'play offices' form a strong contrast to the orderly, modernist corporate interiors that dominated mainstream office design for most of the 20th century. Instead of the usual greys and beiges, play offices feature primary colours and pop-art style prints. Tea rooms and vending machines have given way to espresso bars and micro-kitchens. Break areas have been taken to another level with sports facilities, lounge areas and game rooms. In some cases, the playful nature of the office is directly related to a company's core business. For example, it should come as no surprise that the R&D centre of Lego, the Danish toy company, resembles a children's playground (see page 121). Similar logic applies to the cheerfully designed work settings of companies like Pixar (animation), Disney (entertainment) or Zynga (gaming). In many other cases, however, playful office design is not so much related to a company's products or business processes, but is first and foremost a cultural

Office interior of the gaming company Zynga in San Francisco. There is a neon 'play' sign hanging from the ceiling: play is the core business here. And note the dog: there is a trend among tech companies to allow staff to bring their dogs to the office.

statement intended to express the youthfulness or 'coolness' of the company.

This is especially true for the tech industry where frivolous office design seems to have become the norm. Google is the epitome of this trend. All over the world, Google offices follow a fit-out formula of bold colours, lots of graphics, and lavish amenities—with some local variations, such as the mimicking of an Irish pub in their Dublin office (see page 109) and a tea house in the Tokyo office. To an outsider, the Google offices may seem like the corporate equivalent of Willi Wonka's magic chocolate factory. But at Google they see it as a hallmark of their corporate culture and a logical outcome of the company's overarching philosophy, which is nothing less than "to create the happiest, most productive workplace in the world".[48]

The playful office design of today's tech companies, and of those who want to be like them, can be traced back to the 'dot-com' boom of the early 1990s. At that time, the Internet was a new phenomenon, surrounded by frenzy and immensely high expectations. Numerous so-called dot-com companies emerged to capitalize on the Internet's rapid rise. Many of these companies were started by college-age

Office of the Internet portal Excite, 1998. Excite was probably the first company to feature a slide in its office. The design was by Studios Architecture, which was responsible for many of the brightly coloured Silicon Valley interiors in the 1990s.

entrepreneurs who were eager to break with any rule of conventional business, including those for workplace design. The dominant work ethic was 'work hard, play hard'. People were working ninety hours a week, but also engaging in video games tournaments in the office and playing roller hockey in the car park.

Initially, the offices of dot-com companies were mostly nondescript buildings, filled with cheap cubicles that were hastily acquired to accommodate rapid growth. Silicon Valley was seen as the most innovative place on earth, but it was full of bland office buildings with off-the-shelf interiors. Securing sufficient server capacity was more important than workplace design. But as dot-com companies matured and grew in size, they started to develop their own architectural style: still lots of cubicles, but these were mixed with colourful and casual design features and attractive amenities to compensate for the long work hours.

A good example of a typical dot-com office was the head office of Excite—at the time a major Internet portal. True to Silicon Valley mythology, Excite had been founded in 1994 by a group of former Stanford University students, who used a Palo Alto garage as their

Slide at the Google office in Zurich. This press photo has been used in the numerous articles and blogs about Google's offices, helping the company to portray itself as a fun place to work.

postgrad corporate office. A couple of years later, they had a staff of 230 people and were housed in large shiny office. The interior of the office was organized as a series of 'neighbourhoods' for different teams and departments, which were grouped around a central space—called the 'home page'—where staff could gather and 'hang out'. It was probably the first office ever to feature a slide. Surfboards and bicycles also made their stage appearance as cool office props.

Offices like that of Excite signalled the rapid success, youth and bravura of the dot-com companies—and possibly also their hubris. By the end of the 1990s, the dot-com bubble burst and many companies, including Excite, went bankrupt. For a while, that seemed like the end of the play office. In 2010, *US News* wrote: "In today's lean environment, companies are cutting the superfluities and focusing on getting the job done. If you want to play games, wait till you get home."[49] That judgement proved to be premature, however, at least for the tech industry. In the past few years, the rapid rise of mobile and social media has triggered yet another tech boom. Tech companies are again flush with investor money and competing for talent. And with that, the concept of the office as a corporate playground is being taken more seriously than ever. Not

Miniature golf in the office of the software company Macromedia, 2001. It is a typical example from the first wave of 'fun' office design during first dot-com boom of the 1990s.

only is the slide back (at Google), but so are swings (Box), indoor palm trees (Dropbox), music rooms (Cisco), miniature golf courses (Walmart's online division), video game rooms (SAP) and pool tables (AOL).

These playful offices have received a lot of, mostly enthusiastic, attention in the media. But not all reviews have been positive. Writing in the Internet magazine *Dezeen*, the British designer Sam Jacob dubbed them "places of perpetual adolescence, whose playground references sentence their employees to a never-ending Peter Pan infantilism."[50] A critic in *The Architectural Record* talked of the "infantilizing aesthetic of corporate day care" and commented that such design belittles creative work processes as childish.[51] In similar fashion, *The New York Times* referred to Google's office in New York as "a workplace utopia as conceived by rich, young, single engineers in Silicon Valley".[52]

To a certain extent, these criticisms are probably justified. Many features of the play office come across as attention-seeking gimmicks and décor. After the initial 'wow' moment, the actual value of slides and palm trees becomes questionable. An alternative view, however, is that the play office is a laudable and refreshing attempt to break with the conventions of mainstream office design. Whereas

Miniature golf in the Google office in Dublin, 2013, designed by Camenzind Evolution.

traditional offices tend to be designed according to the principles of hierarchy and efficiency, the play office provides room for amusement, experimentation and irony.

When trying to understand the popularity of the play office in the tech industry, it is important to realize that this industry is extremely dependent on what management consultants call 'human capital'. Tech companies operate in highly competitive, volatile markets. To survive they need to be able to attract and retain best-in-class programmers, brilliant computer engineers and gifted designers. Many of these are young and tech companies do their very best to appeal to them, not only with excellent salaries and more conventional employee benefits, but also with an attractive, almost college-like work environment. From this perspective, the play office is like a recruiting tool that is being used to tell (or rather, shout): "We're cool!" and "This is a great place to work!"

A related explanatory factor is that companies like Google and Facebook have very high revenue per employee ratios. Additional investments in the work environment are easily outweighed by potential productivity improvements—even when such benefits are small and notoriously hard to demonstrate. Seen in this light, sports facilities such as fitness rooms and swimming pools are not luxuries, but rational means of keeping staff fit and healthy and thus productive. The same goes for in-house 'mindfulness' coaches and 'wellness' rooms, which might help valuable programmers to stay fresh. In similar fashion, free restaurants and espresso bars can be seen as essential 'pit stops' where workers can refuel their bodies with high quality caffeine and calories, enabling them to keep up with the high-octane work pace. More practical services, such as laundry and grocery services, ensure that staff do not waste 'their' valuable time on housekeeping errands. According to Google's Eric Smidt. "The goal is to strip away everything that gets in our employees' way... Let's face it: programmers want to program, they don't want to do their laundry. So we make it easy for them to do both."[53]

Employees may consider themselves lucky to have all these perks, but there is also a darker side to it. With free food and leisure facilities on site, there is little need to go anywhere else than the office. Just like in 19th-century company towns, people's lives are to a large extent managed by their employers. In their critical paper *Welcome to the House of Fun*, the British academics Chris Baldry and Jerry Hillier point out that amenities such as games rooms are not merely places to 'chill' during the working day, but also help to entice employees to stay in the office after hours rather than pursuing alternative sites of pleasure and relaxation.[54]

For employers, an important side effect of keeping people at the office is that it can help to enhance social cohesion and camaraderie among staff. Basketball games and Friday beers facilitate the creation of social networks that in turn facilitate the flow of ideas and knowledge within organizations. Companies like Google and Facebook consider such processes as critical to their success. Their offices are designed to promote 'cross-pollination' and 'serendipity', with open-plan workspaces, lots of informal meeting spots and circulation routes that promote chance encounters.

The value that tech companies put on staff interaction is also the reason why they are rather reluctant when it comes to working from home. In the long lists of benefits they offer to their staff, telecommuting is rarely mentioned. Hewlett-Packard and Yahoo went so far as to abandon their existing telecommuting policies. Google, too, is hesitant about the concept. At a conference, the company's CFO remarked that, "The surprising question we get is: 'How many people telecommute at Google?' And our answer is: As few as possible."[55] Rather than letting people work from home, Google prefers to arrange free bus transport from people's homes to the office. And this is obviously one of the ironies of some of the new ways of working: the very tools that allow people to work outside the office, are being developed by people who spend long hours in offices—albeit very playful ones.

Meeting room at Google Dublin. The design of the office is themed, with parts of the interior paying homage to Irish culture. The theme for this meeting room is Irish literature.

GOOGLE, DUBLIN

User: Google
Industry: information technology
Design: Camenzind Evolution, in association with Henry J. Lyons Architects
Location: Dublin, Ireland
Size: 47,000 sq.m./506,000 sq.ft.
Completion: 2013

Google's European head office is located in Dublin's 'Silicon Docks', a former dock area close to the city centre where other tech companies like Facebook, Twitter and Dropbox also have their offices. Google's building is one of the very few high-rises in Dublin. Wrapped in a glazed curtain facade, it looks like an ordinary commercial office building. Inside, however, the building has the cheerful design and the generous amenities that have become a signature feature of the Google identity. There are games rooms, pool tables, micro-kitchens stocked with snacks and an excellent restaurant with free food. There is even a 25-metre swimming pool inside the building.

The office is occupied by over two thousand employees. These 'Googlers', as they are called, are mostly in their twenties and thirties, well educated, casually dressed, and from all over the world. Gorjan Dimitrov is one of them.[56] Originally from Denmark, Gorjan moved to Dublin to work with online marketing at Google, and he explains that he is quite happy being there. The work is interesting and his colleagues are nice and talented. He also notes that the many amenities in the office, like the free restaurant, make his life in Dublin easy, not having to waste too much time on shopping or preparing meals. Regarding the leisure facilities, such as the pool tables, he says: "I don't use them that often, but many do. It depends on how busy you are. If you are facing a deadline, it is not very likely that you will go and play a game of pool. But there many people here, so there is always someone who has time for a game."

The desk areas at Google are not that different from what can be seen in the offices of other organizations: open spaces, furnished with rows of four to six desks. Everybody has his or her own personal desk, often with multiple computer screens on it. There is no clean desk policy. Some of the desks are neat and organized, others are festooned with all sorts of personal items, including toys, flags and cartoons. Gorjan's girlfriend, who also works at Google, has a fishbowl on her desk. One item that is rarely seen on desks is paper. The paperless office is a reality at Google, an impression reinforced by the absence of filing cabinets. To Gorjan this is self-evident: "Everything is digital at Google. Storing paper would be a weird thing to do."

Because everything is digital, the concept of desk sharing could easily be implemented, but for the time being Google is holding fast to the concept of personal workspaces, which is also Gorjan's preference: "I don't see the point of having to search for a desk on a daily basis. It doesn't sound very efficient to spend time on finding out where to sit and where not to."

One of the strategic ideas behind Google's approach to office design is to create an environment that is so attractive that employees like spending time at the office, thereby increasing the chances that people will share ideas and knowledge. According to Gorjan, the strategy is successful. "I can work from home, but I hardly ever do it. At home you miss out on the interaction with your co-workers, which can be critical for your work. Sometimes we come up with an idea during lunch which is so good that we immediately start to test it as soon as we are back at our desks." And that's exactly the type of situation that Google is aiming for. The basic idea behind Google's cheerful office design is that it brings its employees together and creates optimal conditions for collaboration. The Google office may look like a playground, but it is designed to be a very productive playground.

Kitchenette at Google Dublin. At Google, kitchenettes are called 'micro-kitchens', but there is nothing very 'micro' about them. They offer a wide diversity of free snacks, beverages and fruits. There is also enough space for small meetings and get-togethers.

Work area at Google in Dublin. The work areas at Google are dense, with rows of four to six relatively small desks. There is no clean desk policy. Employees are free to decorate their desks as they please.

Hallway at Cisco Meraki. Circulation areas are generous and there are lots of meeting spaces. The aim is to encourage internal communication.

CISCO MERAKI, SAN FRANCISCO

User: Cisco Meraki
Industry: information technology
Design: Studio O+A
Location: San Francisco, US
Size: 10,219 sq.m./ 110,000 sq.ft.
Completion: 2013

In the new Cisco Meraki office in San Francisco, people work everywhere: at their desks, in hallways, on couches, at reading tables, in the coffee bar and on the building's outdoor deck. The building is one big workplace—which is only natural because Meraki's core business is Wi-Fi. The company develops wireless technologies and helps organizations to manage their data networks. Among their better known clients are Stanford University and Starbucks.

The design of the Cisco Meraki office comes from the design firm Studio O+A. In the past ten years, Studio O+A has become the 'go-to' firm for Bay Area tech companies in need of a new office. Casual yet sophisticated, Studio O+A's design style has become the signature look of the tech industry. Their client list includes such well-known tech companies as Facebook and eBay, but also many lesser known start-ups with catchy names such as Zazzle, StubHub and Quid. Designer Primo Orpilla—the 'O' in the firm's name—explains that for the Meraki project, the main challenge was to express the company's identity. When he and his team started working on the project, Meraki had just been taken over by technology behemoth Cisco. Within Meraki this had raised concerns about the potential loss of its own culture, although both companies agreed that it was important to keep the Meraki culture intact—"based out of San Francisco, fun office, free food and all", as Meraki's CEO put it.[57]

Studio O+A's design for the new Cisco Meraki office manages to strike a balance between the corporate maturity of Cisco and start-up 'cool' of Meraki. Raw finishes and inexpensive materials are mixed with designer furniture and fine detailing. Quiet greys alternate with bright hues. Regular open-plan workplaces are flanked by quirky yurt-like structures that function as meeting spots. It is a work environment that is professional, but at the same time very casual— or "dressed down" as Primo Orpilla puts it. The design could also be characterized as playful, but Primo is hesitant about using that term: "Playful design easily regresses into design that is juvenile or arbitrary. We're not interested in that. Our aim is to create workplaces that are welcoming and make people feel at ease."

When asked about mobile work practices, Primo explains that Cisco Meraki was not interested in flexible concepts such as 'hot-desking' or 'desk sharing'. That seems surprising for a firm that works with wireless networks, but according to Primo very few tech companies adopt such concepts. "You would expect young, tech-savvy workers to be at ease with mobile working, and they are, but at the same time they also like to have a home base. So, in most projects we give all workers a personal workstation, but just a small one, and then we create lots of informal areas around it. At Meraki, the desks measure only 30 by 54 inches (76 by 139 cm). This allowed us to create a richness of communal spaces."

In terms of amenities, the Meraki office offers what might be expected of a tech company in San Francisco: a free restaurant with excellent food, a coffee bar with artisan pastries and a professional barista, a game area and an on-site gym. Dogs wander freely between the desks. Employees traverse the large floors on skateboards and scooters. Primo Orpilla explains that the many perks and amenities in the office are the company's way of showing its appreciation of the staff. Besides, some of the perks are simply very practical: "Providing free dinner is not so strange if you take into account that an engineer may start at ten in the morning and then work until midnight. You have to keep in mind that the Meraki office is pretty much a 24/7 space, all year round. With such intense use, it makes good sense to invest in an office that is comfortable and attractive."

Music room at Cisco Meraki. Designer Primo Orpilla: "If a client wants facilities like this, we always warn them that they need to be OK with employees playing guitar at 10 a.m. At Meraki they are."

Work area at Cisco Meraki. The old offices of Meraki featured yurts (Mongolian tents) that were used as meeting spaces. The disadvantage of those yurts was that they provided little acoustic privacy. In the new office, Studio O+A made a contemporary version of the yurts, adding industrial felt for sound absorption.

Meeting table with built-in mini bonsai gardens at Lego PMD. The designers' idea was to play with the notion of scale, which is an essential element of Lego toys.

LEGO, BILLUND

User: Lego PMD
Industry: toys
Design: Rosan Bosch and Rune Fjord
Location: Billund, Denmark
Size: 2,000 sq.m./ 21,528 sq. ft.
Completion: 2010

Lego's product development department is located in Billund, a small town in the West of Denmark. With just over six thousand inhabitants, Billund can hardly be considered a corporate hot spot, but it is the place where Lego was born over a hundred years ago and the company's headquarters and main production facilities are still located there. The development department is housed in an unassuming low-rise building on the corporate campus. The building accommodates over 130 designers and engineers from all over the world, who are responsible for the creation of successful new Lego toys. The office occupies two floors connected by a large, daylight-lit atrium. To get from one floor to the other, staff can go down a shiny tubular slide—although taking the stairs is also an option.

Almost all workspaces in the office are open in order to facilitate communication within and between project teams. Typically, projects teams consist of people from different disciplines—designers, researchers, engineers, marketers—who work closely together. Their desks are placed in groups of four to eight, depending on the size of the project. In between, there are cabinets—mostly filled with Lego objects—that can be rearranged to create space for new projects. Staff interaction takes place across desks, at the various meeting tables in the open workspace and in the brightly coloured conference rooms on the mezzanine floor.

Lego models are everywhere you look: on people's desks, on model-building tables and on display stands that allow Lego developers to show their creations to their co-workers. There is also a 'brick library' where all types of Lego bricks can be found, and playrooms where children are invited to try out prototypes of new toys.

The design of the Lego office is the work of the Danish artists and designers Rosan Bosch and Rune Fjord. Their objective was to develop an environment that would facilitate and stimulate the creative processes of the department. Rosan Bosch explains why the result is reminiscent of a playground rather than a corporate workspace: "We wanted to create an environment where the designers and developers can become part of the children's fantasy world." That may sound fanciful, but Rosan explains that this is Lego's core business: "To create successful new products, Lego's designers need to have an in-depth understanding of how children think, act and play."

One of the most eye-catching elements of the Lego office is the slide connecting the two floors. Rosan Bosch reveals that the slide provoked some discussion during the design process. Some employees were worried that it would lead to too much noise, with people whooping as they went down. Responding to these concerns, she put some extra distance between the slide and the surrounding workstations— although in practice the slide is not a source of much noise. Rosan: "It is not like people are going down the slide all the time. The slide is primarily a symbolic gesture. Its prime purpose is not to transport people from A to B, but to signify playfulness and unconventional ways of thinking, just like the rest of the design."

Looking at this cheerfully designed office, one could argue that while it is a highly suitable solution for a toy company like Lego, it might be less so for other types of companies. Rosan Bosch only partially agrees: "Certain elements are obviously Lego-specific, or even department-specific, but I believe that adding colour and diversity would be beneficial to any work environment. Standard offices tend to be so overly standardized and dull. Their design follows the common denominator: not offending anyone, but not pleasing anyone either. In my opinion, the work environment should be challenging, not boring."

Slide linking the mezzanine to the ground floor of the Lego PMD office. The slide is not just a design gimmick, but a deliberate attempt to create an environment where Lego's designers can connect to the fantasy world of children.

Main workspace at Lego PMD. All workspaces are open, but the space does not feel like a huge open-plan office. Cabinets and 'model towers' divide the space and provide different levels of enclosure for the teams.

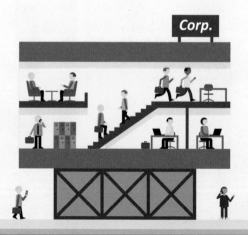

Type 5:
FLEX
OFFICES

Flexible office concepts, with fewer workstations than staff, are becoming mainstream concepts. Office workers are not cheering at the prospect of giving up 'their' desks, but the economic logic behind the concept is hard to argue with. People spend less than of half their working hours behind their desks, so why not share? To be successful, however, the concept should not just focus on reducing the number of desks. The concept is as much about organizational change as it is about workplace design. Staff should be provided with true freedom of choice and management should lead by example.

The traditional desk is dying. That is the belief of the proponents of new ways of working. Workplace expert Philip Ross, for example, states that the idea that people would need "a piece of wood to call their own" will soon become fiction for most companies.[58] The idea is that companies will move away from assigned desks, towards flexible concepts where employees can choose from a diverse mix of shared workspaces. Ross talks of "a sea of choice" and "a landscape of workspaces that suit activities and tasks, personalities and preferences".[59] Some of these workspaces may still be desks, but there will also be cockpits, lounges, hangouts, quiet zones and other exotically named settings.

The idea of the office as an amalgam of shared workplaces is not entirely new. As early as 1970, a group of about twenty IBM product engineers moved, somewhat reluctantly, into what was called a 'non-territorial office'. In their new office, the IBM employees no longer had personal workstations, but could choose from a variety of shared workspaces: normal desks, but also work benches, a quiet area and even a 'total quiet area'—the latter created in the former office of the head of department. Personal items such as pictures had to be taken

'Office of the future' of the Digital Equipment Corporation (DEC) in Finland, 1989. It was one the first non-territorial offices and it received a lot of media attention. One of the novelties was that staff were equipped with cordless telephones.

home. People's own books that were needed for work were purchased by the company and became 'departmental property'.[60]

The aim of the project was to improve the sharing of problems and experience within the department[61]—an ambition that will sound very familiar to all those involved in workplace design today. The assumption was that by abolishing fixed seating, employees would become more mobile, thereby increasing the chances of interaction and knowledge exchange. To test whether this hypothesis was true, the project was evaluated in great detail by researchers from MIT. They followed the non-territorial guinea pigs for a full year, asking them every week about their interactions, and compared their answers to those of a control group in a traditional office.

The survey data showed that the internal communications in the non-territorial office had indeed improved. Combined with a reduced space usage, the project was clearly a success. This came almost as a surprise to the researchers because before the move-in they had noticed that the employees had, at best, mixed feelings about the project. But these feelings shifted in a favourable direction once the group had settled in, with employees volunteering opinions such as "Don't ever fence me in again" and "I was sceptical before, but I'd hate to go back to a closed office now".[62] Based on this observation, the researchers concluded that the non-territorial office was a highly promising concept. Yet they also warned that its implementation should be carefully planned. They noted that the concept could provoke "a good deal of fear or even panic"[63] among users —an observation that is still true today.

The IBM project was an isolated blip in 1970s office design, which did not receive much publicity or any emulation at the time. This lack of attention was not so strange because people were still using electronic typewriters and dial-up corded phones. Work was paper-based and documents were stored in heavy steel filing cabinets. There were computers, but these were large bulky machines that needed to be located in special rooms. All this made the idea of moving around in the office seem highly impractical. This changed in the 1980s and '90s when laptops, Internet and email made their first appearance in the world of work. On the back of these technological advances, the idea of the 'non-territorial office' resurfaced in more glamorous packaging and new names such as 'hot-desking', 'free address offices' or 'hotelling'. Pioneers such as Francis Duffy from the international workplace consultancy DEGW and Franklin Becker from Cornell University presented these concepts as attractive and efficient alternatives to the hierarchical, static and monotonous layouts that had dominated mainstream office design thus far. Early adopters were IT companies and consultancy firms who were practising what they preached. The computer company DEC, for example, opened an 'office of the future' in Finland in 1989 where staff moved around in between easy chairs, fountains, picnic furniture and a swing. DEC's aim was to position itself as a 'cutting edge innovator', showcasing how its technologies could transform work processes. [64]

Many of these early projects were presented as success stories and received lots of media attention. Reality, however, was not always so straightforward. Managers had to be convinced to lead by example and give up their precious corner offices. Office workers had to prepared and taught how to work in a paperless way and keep their desks clean. Extra investments had to be made in technologies such mobile phones, laptops and docking stations and scanners, which were still rare and expensive at that time. Height-adjustable desks came at a premium price.

A notorious illustration of those early difficulties was the New York office of the American advertising agency Chiat/Day. In 1993, Jay Chiat, the founder of company, announced that all walls, desks and cubicles would be disappearing. His ideas were very similar to those behind the early IBM experiment, but the project was more radical, more rushed, and eventually also more troubled. The design was eye-popping, with wild colours, custom-made furniture, and pop-art style features such as Tilt-a-Whirl cars that acted as conversation rooms. The project attracted an immense amount of attention. *Time Magazine* wrote that "the telecommuters of Chiat/Day are among the forerunners of employment in the information age".[65] Large numbers of 'workplace tourists' visited the office on an almost daily basis. But soon enough, the tech magazine *Wired* was able to report that project had gone awry.[66] There were not enough desks, no filing space, and not enough laptops and mobile phones. Employees could not find each other and they could not find a place to work. In 1998, the concept was abandoned.

Today, many of the technological and practical challenges that were faced in these early projects have disappeared. Wireless networks, smart devices, long battery lives and cloud computing have made mobile work easier than ever. Even the paperless office is, at last, coming of age. Office workers no longer have to trail around with 'trolleys' or 'caddies' containing their documents—they can find all they need 'in the cloud'. Just as important: many managers and employees seem to have become used to the concept. Hot-desking was 'hot' in the 1990s, but today it has become the 'new normal' for large numbers of office workers. So, in many ways Chiat/Day was simply ahead of its time. One of the most appealing aspects of the flexible workplace concept has always been its economic logic. It has become received wisdom that traditional desks are heavily underutilized because people are in meetings, on the road, working from home, or on courses, holidays, sick leave, et cetera. Typical desk occupancy figures vary from around 40% to 50%. Such figures make the business case for sharing workspace almost irrefutable. Creating office buildings with empty desks is hard to justify, from both an economic and a sustainability point of view. But the advocates of the flexible office concept are quick to point out that these concepts are not just about space savings. Right from the start, pioneers like Franklin Becker have argued that the primary

Chiat/Day office, New York, 1995. The colourful Chiat/Day office attracted lots of attention, but proved to be too radical, too rushed and too premature. Neither people nor technologies were ready for a virtual and flexible way of working.

goal should be to make people more productive, with costs savings as a secondary, albeit welcome, windfall benefit.[67] The increase in productivity should come from giving staff more control in choosing where, when and how to work—assuming that people have different needs and preferences. In terms of space, this means not just offering fewer desks, but above all a greater diversity of spaces: open offices, quiet rooms, project rooms, phone booths and so on. The appropriate technical term is 'activity-based settings', referring to the idea that there are different types of spaces for different types of activities. The main criticism of flexible office concepts concerns the loss of personal space and territory. Social scientists point out that humans, just like animals, have a tendency towards territorial behaviour, marking and defending spaces as their own in order to create a sense of control and identity.[68] Proponents of flexible working tend to discount such territorial behaviour as petty or 'old ways of working', but in so doing they may overlook its persistence. It is no myth that people arrive early at the office in order to be able to work at their favourite desk. Some people also use jackets, briefcases and papers to claim seats while they are in meetings. Office workers, often managers, have also been known to colonize meeting spaces or quiet rooms as their permanent workspace—which is completely at odds with the concept because it leaves less choice for everyone else.

To counter territorial behaviour, organizations draw up rules and put up signs to remind people of those rules: 'No longer than two hours on this spot', 'No camping' or 'We are quiet here'. Organizations also spend time and money coaching their staff —'defrosting' them and helping them to 'unlearn' their old habits, as consultants like to say. In some instances facility management staff 'police' the space, checking whether clean desk policies are being adhered to.

Such measures can be useful in the initial phases of a project, but they do not bode well if they are required in order to make a concept work in the long term. The trick is to make the concept self-regulating and an integral part of company culture. There should be a sense of 'this is how we do things here', rather than a paper policy. From this perspective, implementing a flexible office concept is much more about organizational change than about physical design. Creating an office with fewer desks and lots of cosy meeting spots is fairly easy. Making people use those spaces as intended is more difficult. This is also why the role of management is critical. For a flexible concept to succeed, managers have to lead by example and keep an eye on the operation of the concept in daily practice. Furthermore, they should give their staff the leeway that is supposed to be part of the concept, looking at their performance rather than their presence at the office.

For individual employees, the acceptance of desk sharing concepts is easier if the new work environment offers a favourable trade-off for the loss of territory. Think of attractive design, advanced IT tools, spaces for quiet work, excellent acoustics and ergonomic furniture. Such features are not only practical and appealing, but they also help make clear that the new office concept is more than just a blunt cost-cutting operation.

An important organizational benefit of non-territorial offices is improved interaction between employees. As the early IBM project showed, internal communications within groups can be improved when people move around. Most research workplace studies confirm this observation, but there are also studies that have raised question marks about how deep these interactions are. In an office project in the UK, sociologist Alison Hirst observed that upon arrival at a chosen desk, people would minimally acknowledge the others sitting nearby, but not

Interpolis office, 1998. The Dutch insurance company Interpolis was one of the first flexible office projects in the Netherlands, conceived by the innovative Dutch office consultant, Erik Veldhoen. The photo shows a woman getting her 'flex suitcase' containing personal stuff out of the 'garage' on her office floor.

introduce themselves for fear of interrupting.[69] According to Hirst, the behaviour seemed comparable to the 'civic inattention' that people display in public spaces: making contact, but also carefully maintaining personal boundaries.

A practical criticism of the flexible office concept concerns the extra hassle that it brings into people's work life. Sharing desks comes with several 'micro-inefficiencies': people have to retrieve personal items from a locker; find an empty desk (thinking about who to sit next to and who to avoid); adjust the found desk and chair to personal preferences; click the laptop into the docking station; put their stuff on the desk; and clean up when they move on. The degree to which all this is truly inconvenient can be debated. Mobile workers, such as sales people and consultants, are already used to working out of their briefcases. People with more sedentary functions may be more resistant to being uprooted again and again. Not surprisingly perhaps, most people in flexible offices tend to stay put at the same desk. Research shows that only 5% of people change workplaces in the course of the day.[70]

In coming years the debate about the pros and cons of the flexible office is likely to continue. Proponents will point to the increasing ease of

Telenor office, 2013. The flexible office comes with behavioural rules. In this Norwegian project, the sign on the walls says: 'We are quiet here'. It signals a 'quiet zone' where phone calls and loud conversations are taboo.

mobile working and the economic and environmental benefits of using less office space. Sceptics will maintain that flexible office solutions are faddish management concepts that are essentially about packing more people into less space. Meanwhile, most users will simply make the best of the situation.

Research does not provide clear conclusions about whether or not flexible office concepts work. Much of what is known about the functioning of flexible offices is case-based and anecdotal. A notable exception comes from the Center for People and Buildings, a Dutch research organization that has evaluated over 87 office projects in the Netherlands, with a total of almost 18,000 respondents. Their research database includes both traditional offices and 'flex offices'. When comparing the two, the researchers of the Center for People and Buildings observed that people in flexible office concepts are slightly less satisfied than those who still have their own desk.[71] The variance, however, is low, and 'covariates' (variables other than the office concept) explain a fair amount of the differences in satisfaction. In particular, people's satisfaction with their own organization appears to play a large role in how they feel about their work environment. In other words: happy workers are more satisfied with their office than unhappy workers—regardless of whether they have their own desk or not.

Locker area in the DSM office. On each floor there are areas for the storage of personal items. They are located close to staircases and elevators, so staff can easily pick up their belongings when entering or leaving the office.

DSM OFFICE, SITTARD

User: Royal DSM
Industry: health, nutrition and materials
Design: Fokkema and Partners (interior)/ Cepezed (building) / ICOP
(workplace concept)
Location: Sittard, the Netherlands
Size: 33,000 sq.m./ 355,209 sq.ft.
Completion: 2011 (first phase)

The large, monolithic office building of DSM is the first thing one notices as one approaches Sittard, a small town in the south of the Netherlands. With over 33,000 square metres of floor space, the building seems too big for the town. The explanation for its being there lies in the past. In 1902, DSM started out as a state-owned mining company, digging up coal reserves in the area. Today, DSM is still there, but it is an entirely different company. Its current business is 'life and material sciences' and it produces a wide array of products, ranging from fibres and plastics, to bio-fuels and nutritional ingredients.

DSM has offices across the world, but the Sittard office is still one of its main nerve centres with over 1,000 people working there. In 2010 it was decided to give the building a major makeover. The building's technical structure was still in good shape, but its interior was worn out. Furthermore, the company felt that the building's traditional office layout, with long corridors and rows of rooms, no longer matched the company's identity as a global, innovative organization. DSM's management decided that the new office should be open and flexible. Instead of having personal desks, staff would share a diversity of workspaces, thereby saving space, but also providing staff with more freedom of choice.

To foster commitment and make sure that the new office would meet the staff's needs, DSM ensured that employees were actively involved in the briefing and design process. Rob Jansen, the project's manager at the time, decided to create a 'concept team' that would be responsible for developing the overall workplace concept. Team members were carefully selected and consisted of ambitious employees of different ages, functions and cultural backgrounds.

The concept team was given three months in which to develop a strategic design brief for the renovation of the building. Inspiration and ideas came from a series of intensive workshops, project visits and briefings from external experts and top management. Rob Jansen: "For me, as the project manager, this approach was a bit of a gamble. When you involve people in such a participative way, it is hard to predict the outcomes. But it proved to be a very productive process. The team presented the new workplace concept to top management and their ideas were well received."

The main hurdle in the project proved to be its scope. Rob Jansen: "The original idea was to tackle the whole building in one go. However, the uncertain economic circumstances led us to opt for a phased approach, renovating the building floor by floor." This approach proved to be advantageous. Employees who were still located on the 'old' office floors could get acquainted with the new way of working by visiting the floors that had already been renovated. Moreover, the project team became wiser with each renovated floor. Rob Jansen: "One of the things we learnt along the way was that the open workspaces were more popular than the enclosed quiet rooms—in contrast to what we had expected—which meant that we could do with less of those. Furthermore, we discovered that the original ratio of seven workstations per ten employees could easily be reduced to six."

Compared to the original interior design, capacity has more than doubled and, according to an evaluation by the Center for People and Buildings, staff satisfaction has increased. So in many ways the project is a success. DSM's challenge now is to find a good use for the resulting surplus space. The local office market in Sittard is small and DSM's need for office space is not likely to increase in the near future. So DSM is thinking about an alternative use for parts of its office space, which could be anything from hotel facilities and educational spaces, to co-workspaces and guest workplaces for DSM's business partners.

Workspace in the DSM office. In the original plan, there were seven desks for every ten employees but actual occupancy measurements showed that a ratio of 6:10 would also work without overcrowding the office.

Workspace in the DSM office. There are open-plan offices, interspersed with small meeting rooms, lounge areas, and rooms for quiet work. All desks are electronically height-adjustable to make it easy to move from one desk to another.

At Telenor, there are 'multirom' (multi-rooms) on all floors. These are small spaces next to the open-plan offices, where people can take phone calls, hold video meetings, do focus work or hold one-on-one meetings.

TELENOR, FORNEBU

User: Telenor
Industry: telecom
Design: NBBJ
Location: Fornebu, Norway
Size: 255,000 sq.m./ 2,744,797 sq.ft. (total building)
Completion: 2002 (original building), 2010-2013 (modifications)

Designing an amazing head office is one thing. Making sure that it is used as intended is another. That is what Telenor has learnt in the ten years since moving into its futuristic head office in Fornebu near Oslo. When Telenor moved into the award-winning building in 2002 it was one of the first companies to embrace the ideas of 'new ways of working' on a grand scale. The building provided 6,000 workstations for over 7,700 people. It featured open workspaces, lots of casual meeting spots and a 'free seating' concept for almost everybody, including the CEO. Wireless networks and laptops allowed the staff to work throughout the building—nothing new today, but at that time quite revolutionary. The project was a big success. The use of space went down from 38 to 21.4 square metres (resp. 409 and 230 sq.ft.) per employee. In a post-occupancy survey, the majority of the staff stated that the building enhanced their productivity. What's more, the survey showed that collaboration among the staff had improved significantly, as intended. Jon Fredrik Baksaas, Telenor's CEO stated: "The number one benefit our campus provides is access to knowledge and other people. I constantly see people teaming up in small informal groups in the atriums and in the meeting areas." The building became a popular destination for 'workplace tourism' and even today, ten years down the track, it still attracts lots of visitors who want to learn about new ways of working. The most important lesson of the project, however, is easy to miss. It is that workplace management is just as important as workplace design. Telenor discovered that without clear ownership and constant care, the concepts of sharing desks and mobile working can easily falter—no matter how fancy the furniture and the technologies. Siri Blakstad, the former head of workplace management at Telenor,[72] explains that when she entered the company in 2010, the flexible workplace concept was exhibiting some cracks: "Much of the organization worked according to the original ideas, but there were also departments where extra desks had been brought in and additional walls had been put up. There were also departments that had shrunk in size, but still made use of the same amount of space, so it actually had a surplus of desks. This is not a problem in itself, but as a technology company Telenor wants to be at the forefront of new ways of working."

According to Siri, ownership of the concept is a critical success factor. "When the project was built, the new workplace concept was very much pushed by top management, which is good. But the telecommunications business is extremely volatile. So, management has many other concerns besides the physical workplace." So it was Siri and her team who took over the responsibility for the concept and made sure that it worked. They carried out new evaluations, tweaked the concept where necessary, developed guidelines, and helped departments to implement the concept, which they now refer to as 'The Telenor Way'. Telenor's workplace team also successfully exported the concept to Telenor's offices abroad. Siri explains: "One might expect a culture clash when implementing such a concept far away from Norway, but it became a big hit, especially in Asia. Even more than in Norway, openness and flexibility is what sets us apart from other employers in these countries. In Pakistan, we were named as most preferred employer. And I am certain that the work environment played a role in that." But Siri Blakstad stresses that there, too, the challenge is to make the concept 'stick', making sure that it works in everyday practice. Summing up her experience, she says: "Moving into a new office is not the end of a change process, but only the beginning. Care, maintenance and management are critical to make a new concept work."

Telenor's meeting rooms are equipped with smart boards and videoconferencing equipment. Telenor operates worldwide and these technologies help to cut down on travel costs and reduce the company's carbon footprint.

WORKPLACES TODAY

Most of the work takes places in the open-plan office. As the photo shows, it is a place where people work at their computers, but also chat, make phone calls and collaborate. If people need quiet to concentrate, they can move to a 'quiet zone'.

The atrium of the GSK office. The atrium is the building's proverbial social heart, with lots of people, light, and sightlines. The prominent maple veneer staircase is intended to encourage employees to use the stairs instead of the elevators.

GLAXOSMITHKLINE, PHILADELPHIA

User: GlaxoSmithKline
Industry: pharmaceuticals
Design: Robert A. M. Stern Architects (building),
Francis Caufmann (interior)
Location: Philadelphia, United States
Size: 19,324 sq.m. / 208,000 sq.ft.
Completion: 2013

The global healthcare company GlaxoSmithKline (GSK) is one of the early adopters of flexible office concepts. For almost a decade now, the company has been experimenting with open and shared workspaces in offices, improving the concept with each new project. Yet GSK's new office in Philadelphia is the company's first building designed and built entirely around the concept of 'SMART working', as it is known in GSK parlance.

Ray Milora is the head of workplace design and change management at GSK. He explains the luxury of creating a project from the ground up: "Most of our earlier projects were in existing buildings where you have to deal with deep floor plans, existing structures and HVAC services that have been laid out on traditional layouts. Making changes in such buildings is expensive and cumbersome. Here, we could make the building as we wished it to be." This resulted in a building with lots of open space, a multitude of informal work settings, a large atrium, a central open staircase, and lots of attention to sustainability.

The objective for the new work environment was to increase both the efficiency and effectiveness of GSK's work processes. Based on occupancy measurements, GSK knew that its old offices were used less than 35% of the time they were available. Creating a more intensively used, shared environment therefore resulted quite easily in significant savings on the lease and on operational expenses such as lighting, cooling, cleaning and maintenance. But Ray Milora prefers not to place too much emphasis on the cost savings. "More important is how the building helps to promote collaboration and break down hierarchical layers within GSK." These benefits are hard to prove, but Milora is certain of the positive impact of the new building. "You should see where we came from. The old building had private offices along the facade and a cube farm in the middle. We were spread over 36 floors. The new building is a total contrast. It is open, filled with light and sightlines. People use stairs instead of elevators and they can work everywhere, even on the roof deck. Communication is easy here."

In the new office, there are around 1,000 sit-stand workstations for 1,300 employees. In addition, there are some 700 informal seats in break areas, the atrium and the restaurant. The chance of everybody being in the office on the same day is close to zero, but if it happens there is still plenty of space. Ray Milora: "This is not an open-plan or hot-desking concept, but a shared environment with a wide mix of settings, ranging from desks and quiet rooms to sofas and meeting rooms. The essential quality is choice."

The office spaces in the building are organized in 'neighbourhoods'. Each neighbourhood consists of around 70 workplaces and accommodates a particular group or department. Milora: "We created the neighbourhoods to provide people with a home base where they can have their locker and find their colleagues. But people are not shackled to their neighbourhood. They can also work elsewhere, for example if they need to collaborate with another department, or if it is too crowded in their own neighbourhood."

To measure the project's success, GSK uses a variety of metrics, such as space efficiency, energy usage, cost per workplace and staff satisfaction. On that last point, Ray Milora is rather sceptical: "Do people like the building? Is 'liking' really an adequate measurement? Most important is that it works." Having said that, Milora proudly adds that a recent post-occupancy evaluation of the building shows that 85% of the staff are satisfied.

To maintain the success, Ray stresses the importance of continuous change management. "Most people quickly get used to the new way of working, but you can also see old habits slipping back in." Management's role is critical in keeping the concept alive. Managers have to lead by example and discuss the concept with their staff. Moreover, Ray Milora stresses that managers should focus on people's performance rather than their presence at the office: "The concept falls apart if a manager want see his people at their desks, all day and every day." But he is not afraid that this will happen. "It just doesn't work like that anymore."

Open meeting space, with lockers in the background. The GSK office is divided into 'neighbourhoods' for specific departments and teams, each with their own meeting spaces, desk space, quiet rooms and locker areas.

Workspaces at GSK. The photo shows that some desks are quite cluttered. However, GSK's clean-desk policy requires employees to remove all items before going home. According to GSK, this has contributed to a 90% reduction in paper use.

Type 6:
STUDIOS

Studios are workspaces that are part office, part atelier and part workshop, typically used by firms working in architecture, fashion and design. They are places where creative professionals spend long hours, often working in teams on very tangible projects and products. Studios also tend to be very 'material' and revealing environments. Large work tables carry computers, as in ordinary offices, but also prototypes, models, sketch books, printouts, and material samples. The atmosphere is creative and collaborative—qualities that are much sought after by other types of organizations as well.

The origins of the studio type lie in the Renaissance when the term studio was used to refer to the workshop of an artist specializing in the fine or decorative arts. In those times, a studio was a place where a principal master and a number of assistants and apprentices worked together on pieces that went out in the master's name.[73] It was also a place where juniors came to learn skills and competences, learning by doing and being taught by the master—hence the term studio, which comes from the Latin *studere*, which means 'to study' or 'zeal'.[74]

An engraving by the Flemish artist Jan van der Straet from around 1590 provides a naturalistic impression of a Renaissance studio. The master painter is the central figure. Around him are other painters working on smaller pieces, pupils preparing palettes, workers grinding pigment and a delivery boy bringing in new material. Van der Straet's depiction is interesting because it does not show the studio as the idealized 'clean' atelier of a solitary artist, but as a messy and busy workshop, filled with activity and collaboration, organized according to clear hierarchical lines.

Today's studios are not so different. Graphic design studios, architecture practices, fashion houses and other creative businesses

Engraving of a Renaissance studio, made by Philips Galle after Jan van der Straet, circa 1590. It shows the studio as a busy place of artistic production, with a clear hierarchy between the master and his pupils.

also tend be organized around signature designers who are supported by juniors, assistants and project managers. Work tends to be done in teams and learning takes place on the job. Signature designers act simultaneously as managers, teachers and arbiters of quality, deciding whether the produced outcomes are good enough to go out under the firm's name.

As in Jan van Straet's engraving, the beating heart of the studio is usually an open workspace that accommodates a myriad of activities. The studio of the architect Frank Gehry in Santa Monica is a good example. It is a cavernous space filled with large work tables that are strewn with Perspex models, computers, folders, product catalogues, plotted drawings and sketches. Some of the designers are in conversations. Others are focusing on their large computer screens. It is a busy production space, intensely used for thinking, experimentation, discussions and computer modelling. In an interview, Frank Gehry had this to say about his studio: "Well, this is not a buttoned-down corporate office. It's like an artist's studio. Models all over the place. It's worked in. Lived in."[75]

The openness of studio spaces is strongly connected to their function

Gehry studio in Santa Monica. Architects, designers, project managers, model makers and assistants are at work on projects at various stages of completion. (photo: Martin Crook)

as places for learning. Following the classic apprenticeship model, juniors learn the 'tricks of the trade' on the work floor. To outsiders, these learning processes may not always be very visible. The studio atmosphere may strike visitors as hushed and studious, with people quietly working at their computer, wearing earplugs to block out the outside world. But at frequent intervals, the silence is likely to be punctured by ad hoc design meetings, with people standing around a computer screen or scale model, reviewing work-in-progress with chief designers and colleagues. Part of the learning process is a matter of simply being aware of what is going on, listening in to conversations and seeing the work of others.

Another reason for the openness of the studio lies in the need for coordination. Complex design assignments, such as architectural or product design, tend to involve a multitude of disciplines and tasks that are social and collaborative in nature.[76] The activities of team members are often interdependent and the relationships between people dynamic. People are working together on various projects in different constellations, often under the pressure of deadlines. In such cases, being close to one other in the same space aids the integration of tasks. Quick overview and easy accessibility are critical for project coordinators who rush around communicating design changes and helping to solve ad hoc problems and checking design work in various stages of completion.[77]

The importance of learning, collaboration and coordination is probably also the reason why concepts such as telework (or telecommuting) have never really taken off in the creative industries. Lead designers and project managers tend to be very mobile, spending lots of time travelling, visiting clients and attending project meetings, but the bulk of the production work is done at the studio where design teams work on details, renderings, samples and presentations. Working long hours (including nights and even weekends) at the office is rule rather exception. There are no figures available, but the intensity of use of studios spaces is bound to be higher than that of ordinary offices.

Another significant characteristic of the studio is its workshop-like character. As in ordinary offices, most of the work takes place on computers. Drawing boards have long since been replaced by large computer screens and advanced design software. Yet, in many cases, design work still entails the use of very tangible materials and production tools. Fashion designers work with fabrics and are likely to have a dedicated sewing room. Product designers construct physical prototypes with 3D printers and laser cutters. Graphic designers are likely to make prints of their work and may still sketch on paper. In architecture, so-called building information models (BIM) are all the hype, but producing physical models is still an important part of the design process. The Gehry studio is again a good example: the designers there use highly advanced design software, but they also experiment with scale models made out paper, cardboard and other materials. Gehry is also famous for walking around the office looking for objects that might be just the right size for a model in progress—Perrier bottles and apples have ended up in his models.[78]

The material nature of design work processes leaves its traces in the studio space. Tables may hold scale models and prototypes. Desks are liable to be cluttered with prints, magazines, colour coding charts, drawing pencils and material samples. Walls may be covered with photos, sketches, artist's impressions and diagrams. A well-known example of such a 'rich' studio environment is the Eames office— one of the most influential design studios of the 20th century. Photographs

Interior of the Eames studio in Venice, California in the 1970s. Max Underwood, a former Eames employee, described it as a "tsunami of visual, sensual and emotional stimuli" and a "cacophony of inspirational design artifacts."[82]

of the studio of Ray and Charles Eames taken in the 1970s reveal a work environment crammed with prototypes, books, clippings, and 'found objects' that served as inspiration. In an interview, Ray Eames explained: "We found things and kept them as examples of principles or aspects of design. We kept it to show it, to use it, to share it, to give insight to others and to ourselves. We would say 'that is a great example of...' whatever it was."[79]

As the quote from Ray Eames indicates, the paraphernalia often found in studios can be seen as instrumental objects that allow designers to discuss, criticize and explore new possibilities in their work. The scientific term for this is 'cognitive artefacts', which are objects that aid or enhance people's cognitive abilities, acting as reminders, sources of inspiration or storage space for ideas.[80] It has also been argued that visible displays and tangible artefacts help create a greater degree of shared awareness within project teams, helping to 'anchor' the understanding and contribution of individual team members.[81]

Some studies even suggest that 'creative clutter' helps to stimulate creativity. The American psychologist Kathleen Vohs conducted an experiment in which she asked two groups of students to come up with

Interior of the Bungie gaming studio. It is a dense, hectic place. Each game developer has three computer screens. There are high windows, but the curtains are drawn to avoid glare and sun reflection.

new uses for ping-pong balls to help a manufacturer. One group was put in a clean, neat room, the other in a disorderly room with lots of clutter. This last group generated more highly creative ideas than did participants in the orderly room. Vohs and her research team concluded: "Disorderly environments seem to inspire breaking free of tradition, which can produce fresh insights ... Orderly environments, in contrast, encourage convention and playing it safe."[82]

It should be said that not all studios conform to the romantic image of a workshop filled with creative clutter. Studios can also be neat, minimalistic, austere spaces. There may be materials on desks and drawings on the wall, but in many studios the atmosphere is understated and neutral. Usually there are wide open workspaces, with no other colours than white and grey. Interiors with bare concrete floors, basic strip lighting and exposed ducts are more popular than cosy or sleek office settings.

Designers may opt for a raw and austere look because they want to have a blank backdrop for their work. The architect Florian Idenburg, who designed the Derek Lam fashion studio in New York (see page 167), suggests that if a firm works with tangible products such as clothing,

Collaboration in the Bungie studio. Open spaces allow for ad hoc problem-solving and collaboration with colleagues.

there is no need for additional texture or colour in the office. Another reason may be that studio spaces reflect particular ideas about creativity. In mainstream management literature, creativity is often associated with playfulness, but designers are more likely to regard it as a serious skill. They view it as an integral part of their work process, something that takes place on the work floor, rather than a special sort activity that needs be 'teased out' in brainstorming rooms with funny furniture.

Deviations from the serious studio look can be seen in 3D animation and game design studios. There, the design approach is less 'cultural' and more entertainment driven, with more room for playful design. The essentials of the studio model, however, remain very much the same, with open, dense and messy workspaces. A good example is the studio of the game developer Bungie (creator of the science fiction game Destiny), which accommodates over 350 people. The Bungie studio looks like a darkened version of the Gehry studio: there are no scale models, but it has the same frenetic, beehive-like atmosphere.

The studio model is interesting because it is strongly associated with creativity, which is a hot topic in today's management thinking. What was once called the 'knowledge economy' is now frequently referred to as the 'creative economy'. The idea is that it is not only designers and artists who are dependent on creative thinking, but also software developers, lawyers, policymakers and others working in areas where success depends on good ideas.[83] As such, it is hardly surprising that 'normal' offices are starting to look more and more like design studios. In the corporate world, the trend is to replace cubicles and corner offices with wide open spaces with communal work tables. Carpets and false ceilings are taken out to expose the building's construction elements and create the sought-after 'creative look'. Whether such changes will indeed make the inhabitants of these spaces any more creative obviously remains to be seen. The essence of the studio model lies not so much in its physical appearance, but in the idea of gathering together a group of talented people and putting them in a place where they can work hard, collaborate, and learn from one another—just like in the original Renaissance model.

Derek Lam's own office consists of a simple white desk and a classic Eames aluminium chair. There is a clothes rack with his latest designs and bolts of fabric in the far corner.

DEREK LAM, NEW YORK

User: Derek Lam International LLC
Industry: fashion design
Design: SO-IL (Solid Objectives – Idenburg Liu)
Location: New York, United States
Size: 1,000 sq.m. / 11,000 sq.ft.
Completion: 2009

Derek Lam is a celebrated American fashion designer based in New York. His award-winning work is popular among the well-off, celebrities, and fashion lovers across the world. Fashion critics describe his style as sophisticated, simple, modern and 'understated chic'.

The same terms can be used to describe the design of his studio workspace in SoHo, New York. The studio is spread over the three floors of a classic cast-iron loft building. Previously used as a boxing gym, the building was turned into a fashion studio by the architecture firm SO-IL. The architects stripped the interior down to its bare essentials and created a light, basic, almost pristine workspace with only a few judicious architectural elements. Almost all surfaces are white except for a dark wooden floor and a long reflective wall that runs through the whole building. True to New York's loft style, ceilings are high with exposed sprinkler installations and electricity ducting. Basic strip lighting is used to light the spaces.

With its low-key, minimalist features, SO-IL's design does not impose itself. The almost austere environment provides a neutral backdrop for Derek Lam's design work. Architect Florian Idenburg, one of the principals of SO-IL, explains: "In general I don't believe that creative work needs to happen in overly tactile environments, and in the case of Derek Lam it is the clothing that provides texture and colour to the office." And indeed, the space could not be mistaken for anything other than a fashion studio. There are computer workstations as in an ordinary office, but also bolts of fabric, fashion drawings, racks of dresses and shirts, samples and magazines. On one of the three floors, there is a sewing room with workstations for cutting and sewing fabric, and a large pattern printer. In the entrance area, there are slender young women waiting to act as live mannequins for Derek Lam's new creations.

The office areas of the studio are a mix of open and enclosed spaces. Florian Idenburg: "The design brief stated that the space had to be open, but it also had to provide a degree of privacy. This seemingly contradictory demand had to do with the diverse nature of the activities that had to be accommodated: design work, of course, but also administration, the production of samples and prototypes, model casting, press conferences and sales." To deal with this dual request for openness and privacy, SO-IL created a series of adjoining spaces that are separated by walls, but connected through large 'portals' or wall openings. According to the architect: "The portals form a soft definition of the respective realms where the different activities of the organization take place."

Derek Lam's own workspace is just as basic as all the other spaces in the building: whitewashed brick walls, strip lighting and large windows with painted radiators underneath. There are bookshelves containing art and fashion books. There is a classic Eames office chair and a simple white desk with a few papers and a laptop. As the head of an international firm, Derek Lam spends a lot of his working hours away from this office—travelling from meeting to meeting and from show to show. Yet the studio remains an important workplace for him. As he explained in an interview with *Vogue*: "I draw anywhere I get inspired. Any scrap of paper is fine. But usually, I just turn on some music and sketch at my desk and hope I can get a few sketches into work before heading to yet another meeting." [85]

Reception area in Derek Lam's studio. Mannequins are waiting to try out new creations—certainly not a common sight in normal offices.

Workspace at Derek Lam's studio. It has all the traits of a typical studio space: a bare brick wall, a long work table, basic strip lighting and 'creative clutter', such as clothing samples and printouts.

The main workspace at Mamastudio. A graphic designer is slouched in his chair, concentrating on his screen, while his co-workers chat.

MAMASTUDIO, WARSHAW

User: Mamastudio
Industry: Visual communication
Design: Mamastudio
Location: Warsaw, Poland
Size: 100 sq.m. / 1076 sq.ft.
Completion: 2007

The idea for setting up Mamastudio arose over ten years ago when its three founders were sitting on a park bench discussing how to avoid taking corporate jobs they considered draining, boring and entirely uncreative. The only way to achieve full creative freedom, they decided, was to become their own employers. And so they founded Mamastudio and started to work out of a tiny, sub-leased basement space with three second-hand Macs and a lot of zeal and enthusiasm.[86]
Today, Mamastudio is an award-winning design studio, ranked as one of Poland's most creative firms. Having consciously remained independent and small, the studio now has a staff of eight and is housed in an old, slightly dilapidated building in central Warsaw.
The studio comprises a large open workspace with a separate kitchen and a meeting room which is called 'the aquarium'. "Working together in the same space can be challenging, but it works," says Erik Hurless, design director at Mamastudio. "It never gets chaotic or distracting. Most client meetings happen outside of the studio, but a few times a week we'll conduct various types of meetings in the aquarium. Music fills the whole space and it's rare that someone disconnects from the rest by putting on headphones. We've managed to cultivate a creative working environment that is neither quiet nor distracting. It's comfortable."
The openness also fits the general atmosphere, which is very casual. The staff go round in T-shirts, faded jeans and hipster sneakers. Desks are littered with printouts, soft drink cans, markers, pencils, empty coffee cups and magazines. The furniture is a mishmash of cheap IKEA products and vintage design objects. The walls and the sides of cabinets are adorned with posters and drawings. One of the walls sports a neon sign from an old bar. On another wall is an stuffed deer's head.

Erik Hurless points out that this atmosphere of 'creative messiness' is not something they have deliberately created. "The nature of what we do decorates our space spontaneously. There is very little effort in it ... Many of the things lying around our studio are necessary tools to help us do our work. Some things may be there to serve as an unconscious source of inspiration. The semi-eclectic atmosphere just seems to 'happen'—we don't control it." In addition, Erik believes that it is an expression of their way of working: "Part of what we do is analytical, practical and strategic. Another part is artistic, creative and sometimes silly. The space reflects both aspects of our personality."

The intensity of use of the studio is high. The firm tries to maintain normal office hours and to avoid working at weekends, but as in any design studio deadlines often dictate the work schedule and they can spend many extra hours in the studio when necessary. This makes the studio an important place in the life and work of the Mamastudio staff. Asked about whether people also work from home, Erik answers that the studio is the preferred workplace. "The studio is definitely the dominant place for work. We're a team and our workspace caters to, and enhances, the benefits of teamwork. It's a place we each come to every day to integrate, communicate and create."

Meeting table at Mamastudio. The table is just large enough to accommodate all studio members. A fan in the corner of the room helps to keep the space comfortable during summer.

The main workspace at Mamastudio. White bookshelves containing art books, design magazines and project documentation in folders create a degree of separation between the desks.

Entrance to MAD's main studio space. The wall behind the copying machine is covered in A3 printouts of a design proposal for a luxury hotel in Dubai.

MAD ARCHITECTS, BEIJING

User: MAD Architects
Industry: architecture/design
Design: MAD
Location: Beijing (China)
Size: 800 sq.m. / 8,611 sq.ft.
Completion: 2005 (interior)

MAD Architects is an award-winning architecture firm, based in Beijing. The firm is known for its futuristic design style with flowing lines and eye-catching curves. The founder of the firm is the Chinese architect Ma Yansong.

He is just under forty, but already an internationally acclaimed 'starchitect'. In 2014, the American magazine *Fast Company* listed him among the top 100 most creative people in business. Together with two partners, he heads up a studio of about eighty people.

Despite its fame and success, MAD is still located in the same humble building where it started out in 2005. It is a rather nondescript, grey building, located in an alleyway of one of Beijing's traditional hutong neighbourhoods. MAD occupies the building's two upper floors. Inside, the spaces are open, with whitewashed walls, bare brick walls and white epoxy floors. Light comes from naked fluorescent tubes attached to the wooden beams that support the roof. Basic white desks are occupied by young architects from across the world, working at large computer screens. The back wall of the studio is one large bookshelf, filled with black binders containing project documentation. Recently, some large green plants were added, bringing a touch of colour into the otherwise all-white spaces.

The modesty of the studio space seems to contrast sharply with MAD's ultramodern, sleek design style and the grand projects that are dreamed up here. But according to Tammy Xie, press officer at MAD, the contrast is not as big as it seems. "The set-up of our studio is simple, but it's spacious, light, well-equipped and designed around the staff's needs. As in our projects, we try to follow the Chinese notion of 'Shan-Shui', which is about harmony between nature, humanity and architecture. It is also about integrating traditions and new developments, so it is not so strange that we are in an old building." She adds that the firm sees its staff as its main asset, so they try to make the work environment as pleasant as possible. And it seems to work. "We simply love this space," says Tammy Xie.

The studio's main workspace is large and open. Here, interns, project managers, designers and the firm's principals all work side-by-side. Tammy explains that the openness helps to create a sense of belonging and allows easy communication. In addition, it brings a certain dynamism to the studio. People are working, chatting, having meetings, walking in and out. "I would say it's busy, but not noisy ...There are always things happening, but not in a crazy or undisciplined manner." The dynamics of the MAD studio are reflected in the project materials that are all over the studio. Some desks are pristine, but many of them are covered in papers and coffee cups. Large tables in the middle of the workspace carry scale models of twisted skyscrapers and mushroom-like building structures. Walls are covered in printouts of renderings, floor plans and photos of the firm's projects. Tammy explains that the drawings and models are used for internal design discussions, but also for exhibitions and for explaining the firm's work to the continuous stream of visitors—clients, students, designers and journalists.

The abundance of project material is also evidence of the firm's work load. MAD is 'hot', which translates into lots of projects and lots of deadlines. MAD's normal office hours are from half past nine in the morning to half past seven in the evening, but it is not unusual for staff to have to work late in the evenings or at weekends. "This is not a nine-to-five office," notes Tammy. She emphasizes, however, that the firm's ethos is not about work only. Many of the MAD staff are young and the atmosphere is jovial and friendly. A visible sign of MAD's informal culture is the firm's ping-pong table, which is much used during breaks, by staff and principals alike. Tammy says: "We're creative, hard-working MAD'ers, but we know how to make our work environment a friendly and fun place."

One of MAD's many young architects working at her computer.

Interior of the main workspace at the MAD studio. A large table with design models stands in the centre of the studio space. There is an interesting contrast between these elegant, futuristic shapes and the 'raw' and basic character of the studio space where they are produced.

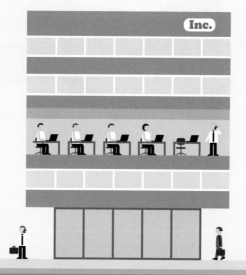

Type 7:

MODERNIST OFFICES

Modernist offices are classic 20th-century offices: large boxy buildings made out of steel, concrete and glass, designed for both efficiency and prestige, with travertine lobbies and gridded office floors. The work environments inside these buildings are a composition of open plans, false ceilings, raised floors, movable partitions and systems furniture. The design expression is orderly, neutral and organized. These buildings are pure offices: streamlined machines for working in, without any intention to be playful, cosy or casual.

Modernist offices are the stereotypical kind of office one sees in movies and comic books: large glazed buildings, with shiny lobbies and stacks of generic office floors, populated by men and women in neat business attire. On the office floors, large numbers of identical desks are positioned on efficient, Cartesian grids, not wasting a centimetre of valuable space. The floors are large and open—referred to as 'universal plans'—offering a maximum of flexibility, efficiency and overview. Fit-out components such as movable partitions, false ceilings and raised floors are modular and mass-produced. The materials and finishes are glossy and smooth. All is rectangular, organized and clean. The design rules for this type of office were developed in the early 20th century by modernist architects who wanted to build technologically advanced, progressive, unornamented buildings. In 1923, the German architect Ludwig Mies van Rohe—the high priest of corporate modernism—wrote: "The office building is a house of work, of organization, of clarity, of economy. Broad, light workspace, unbroken, but articulated according to the organization of the work. Maximum effect with minimum means. The materials: concrete, steel, glass."[87] Three decades later, Mies van der Rohe was able to put these words into practice when he was commissioned to design the head office of the Canadian liquor company Seagram in New York. The Seagram Building was a high-rise office tower with 38 storeys of generic office space, wrapped in black-tinted glass sheets that were held in place by bronze mullions. In architectural history, the building is seen as one of the purest examples of corporate modernism. A *New York Times* critic described it as "the millennium's most important building".[88]

A somewhat lesser known, but perhaps even more influential example of corporate modernism was the Union Carbide Building in New York, dating from the same period. This building was by designed by the American firm Skidmore, Owings & Merrill (SOM), which went on to become one of the largest architectural practices in the world. *Fortune* magazine wrote: "SOM took Mies's stainless steel standard, warmed it up and sold it as a prestige package to the US businessman."[89]

SOM's design of the Union Carbide Building is interesting because the firm applied modernist principles not only to the building's structure and facade, but also to the work environment. The office interiors were an exercise in rational and precise space planning. The suspended, luminous ceiling, movable partitions, and partial-height privacy partitions achieved a level of integration that set a new standard for the development of interior systems.[90] Photographs of the building's interior, with rows of desks neatly arranged beneath luminous ceiling panels, became icons for the corporate world of the mid 20th century.

The 1950s and '60s were the epoch of corporate modernism, but the ideas and aesthetics are still very much present. Corporate modernism has developed into the vernacular of office architecture, dominating business districts across the world—its design formula not much changed by local culture, time or climate.

A perceptive description of a contemporary modernist office environment can be found in the book *The Pleasures and Sorrows of Work*, by the Swiss-British pop philosopher Alain de Botton, who describes his visit to the office of a large accountancy firm located in Canary Wharf, London. The building, De Botton notes, was "oddly clean" and "assembled out of steel frames, sheeted in simple tinted glass". Inside, "everything in the accountant's building appears elegant and well-maintained. There are none of the cobwebs endemic to the ordinary world". He also mentions "the expansive

Interior of the Union Carbide Building, 1960. The Union Carbide Building was a prototype of modular, rationalized office design. Its design principles would be replicated and copied throughout the world during the following decades.

regularity of the open plan arrangement where desks are identified only by stark acronyms like Ml6W.246."[91]

In some ways, De Botton could have been describing SOM's Union Carbide Building from six decades earlier. There is the same impression of cleanness, regularity and efficiency. At the same time, however, there are fundamental differences. The desks, for example, may seem quite similar—rectangular, horizontal work surfaces, neatly positioned on a rectangular grid—but the artefacts on top of them— typewriters, Bakelite dial phones, rolodexes, ashtrays—have long since disappeared from contemporary office life.

Furthermore, there is a marked difference in organizational and spatial hierarchy. In offices like the Union Carbide building, the staff's status and rank were indicated by the size and location of their office, the number of windows in that office, and the refinement of its furnishings.[92] Luxurious executive floors and expansive corner offices for managers were the rule rather than the exception. Today, such ostentatious status markers are frowned upon as corporate hierarchies have flattened and society has become more egalitarian— even though it would be a mistake to suggest that hierarchy has

Interior of Markit, a financial services firm in London, 2011. In terms of design, this contemporary interior is quite similar to that of the Union Carbide office of 1960. However, the work processes are entirely different: no female clerks, but highly paid, male financial traders, working with advanced computer systems instead of typewriters.

disappeared altogether. The CEO of the accountancy firm De Botton visits, sits in the middle of a regular floor at a desk no different from that of an intern, thereby expressing a culture of egalitarianism, although De Botton also notes that "of course, power has not disappeared entirely; it has merely been reconfigured. It is by posing as a regular employee that the chairman stands the best chance of preserving his seniority".[93]

The most fundamental difference concerns the work processes that take place inside these buildings. The offices of the mid 20th century housed large administrative departments and typing pools where office staff, mostly women, carried out repetitive administrative tasks. Secretaries, typists and clerks were responsible for keeping and creating records, correspondence, and administration. Today, many of those activities have been automated. The work that remains is of a more complex and creative nature. The 'white collar proletariat' of clerks and typists has been replaced by 'knowledge workers' and members of the 'creative class', who tend to operate in much more informal, collaborative and autonomous ways. These new breeds of office workers may still work in open-plan offices, but the openness has taken on a different meaning. In the age of the Union Carbide Building, open spaces were an expression of efficiency, control and hierarchy. These days, openness is presented as a token of progressiveness and a means to promote collaboration and team work.

In particular, professional bureaucracies such as banks, insurance companies, accountancy firms and government organizations seem to have retained a fondness for what architects lovingly call 'Miesan' aesthetics. Such organizations have to house large numbers of staff and their work processes need to run smoothly and efficiently— characteristics that still seem to go well with the orderly design expression of corporate modernism.

A less obvious example of corporate modernism can be found in the design for the new head office of Apple, generally considered one of today's most innovative firms. The company's new office is being designed by the eminent British architect Norman Foster. The building has not been built yet, but Foster's plans show an unmistakably modernist building with a close resemblance to the minimalist design of Apple's products. The architectural critic Aaron Betsky noted disapprovingly that it is "the kind of building Skidmore, Owings, and Merrill would have designed in their heyday: meticulously detailed, polished to within an inch of its life, modular and repetitive, and without any quirks, exceptions, or sense of human scale or presence."[94] The case of Apple is interesting because Foster's high-tech design style is the very opposite of the playful, quirky office design that can be seen at Google, Apple's main competitor (see page 109). Both companies operate in the same market and share much of the same genius, but their buildings reflect strong differences in the corporate culture and the personal preferences of their founders. It is perfectionism versus experimentation, seriousness versus irony, and sleekness versus geekiness.

Critical commentators tend to regard corporate modernism as sterile and bleak. Modernist architects have been criticized for being "more interested in the formal possibilities of reflective glass than any real organizational requirements or actual developmental possibilities."[95] In *The Rise of the Creative Class*, Richard Florida refers to traditional corporate spaces as "obsessively neat and regular, and often subdued to the point of blandness". He suggests that today's creative workers are in need of more visually arresting, raw environments, mentioning bold colours, wall-sized art works and exposed pipes and beams.[96]

Rendering of the new Apple office in Cupertino, designed by Norman Foster. There has been a lot of debate about Foster's design proposal for Apple's head office. Its clean design and meticulous detailing prompted architectural critic Aaron Betsky to call it 'Modernism on valium'.[101]

Elsewhere, corporate modernism has been described as an "idealized aesthetic form ... devoid of human emotion, human clutter, human irregularity, and human 'messiness' in any form."[97]

It is all too easy, however, to make a stereotype out of corporate modernism. It is true that business parks all over the world are filled with mediocre glass boxes (the American architect Philip Johnson is said to have quipped that Mies van der Rohe was such a good architect because he was easy to copy[98]). But there are also sophisticated modernist office buildings that offer their users light, calm and elegant work environments. One example is the new office of the Danish bank Nykredit in Copenhagen (see page 195), designed by the Danish architecture firm Schmidt hammer lassen. In essence, this building is another 'glass box', but it is carefully designed, with lots of attention to user comfort and sustainability. The office floors are of a limited size and offer abundant daylight and attractive views out to all workstations in the building. The abundant use of steel and glass is offset by wooden flooring which gives the building a warm feel. The overall image is crisp and calm rather than funky or fashionable.

Companies like Nykredit do not want to appear hip or progressive, but

'Getting Up' by Hariton Pushwagner, 2010. Pushwagner's work presents a dystopian image of the modernist office as a white-collar factory, populated by identical men, seated behind rows of identical desks, under harsh fluorescent lighting.

rather trustworthy, efficient and professional. Corporate modernism still seems capable of expressing those values. Part of the appeal may also lie in the neutral and generic character of modernism, which makes it a safe choice for large organizations with a lot of staff and a lot of clients.[99] The American design critic Thomas Hine observed that office workers may like neutral design "because they recognize that if a strong taste is expressed in the space, it won't be theirs. More likely, it will be that of a top executive who confuses his own quirks with the personality of the entire company."[100]

The ultimate quality of corporate modernism may be its straightforwardness. It is an 'honest' design style in the sense that it explicitly strives for efficiency and effectiveness. There are desks, meeting spaces and a possibly impressive lobby—but no slides, village squares or cosy living rooms or other elements intended to disguise that offices are places for work. The modernist office is the office as the office and does not pretend to be anything else.

Entrance of the Nykredit office. A generously designed wooden staircase leads up to the building's reception floor. The impressive and 'chic' atmosphere befits a building that accommodates Nykredit's private banking operations.

NYKREDIT, COPENHAGEN

User: Nykredit
Industry: financial services
Design: Schmidt hammer lassen architects.
Location: Copenhagen, Denmark
Size: 6,850 sq.m./73,732 sq.ft.
Completion: 2011

Nykredit's most recent addition to its corporate campus in the centre of Copenhagen is known as the 'Crystal', a reference to the building's angular shapes and shiny facades. The building stands next to the bank's headquarters, dubbed the 'Cube', completed ten years earlier. Both buildings were designed by the Danish firm Schmidt hammer lassen architects, which is known for its simple yet elegant modernist architecture—and an evident fondness for basic geometrical shapes. The Crystal is home to Nykredit's private banking unit, which serves the bank's top clientele. It is a function that is well-matched by the chic, jewel-like expression of the building, but the architects did not know this beforehand. Kim Holst Jensen, partner at Schmidt hammer lassen architects, says: "When we got the commission, there was actually no clear design brief. The bank was growing and in need of extra space. But they didn't know yet who would be housed in the building. Their key requirement was to make it very, very flexible."

This requirement translated into a building with raised floors, movable walls, and technical services with lots of extra capacity. In a matter of days, office floors can be changed from cellular layouts with private offices, to fully open-plan spaces and even dealing rooms. Moreover, the building's set-up is such that floors could easily be rented out should the bank no longer have need for the space.

The building's interior consists of Z-shaped floors that are positioned around two triangular atria. The atria bring daylight deep into the building and generate sightlines across all floors. The fit-out of the office floors is what one would expect of high-end Danish office design: spacious open work areas, wood floors, lots of glass and plenty of Arne Jacobsen furniture.

Commenting on the openness of the workspaces, Kim Holst Jensen remarks: "Ten years ago, when our firm worked on the design of the Cube, open workspaces were still a new thing in Denmark. It raised a lot of discussion as many people were still working in cellular offices. Today, however, open plans have become part of the bank's policy and the same goes for most other Danish companies. People don't expect anything different". It is important to point out, however, that it is openness on a modest scale. Floor plates are fairly small. No workstation is further than nine metres away from the triple-glazed facade, ensuring that all staff can benefit from daylight and views out. Desks are grouped in configurations of no more than four, with semi-high filing cabinets in between. As in other Scandinavian offices, all workstations are furnished with electronically adjustable sit-stand desks.

As always with open-plan offices, acoustics were a key consideration. Because of the extensive use of glass and the timber flooring, there was a danger of noise and reverberations—from people talking and from the click-clack of the leather soles and high heels of the neatly dressed Nykredit staff. To avoid this, ceilings were fitted out with perforated steel panels lined with sound absorbing material. In addition, the sides of the atria were clad with acoustic panelling. Because the atria are open to the work floors, sound can still travel from one floor to the other, but it is mostly a soft kind of 'buzz' that helps to mask the sounds of private conversations and phone calls on the work floors.

The aesthetic expression of the building's interior is calm and neutral, with white desks and black chairs, neatly arranged in an orderly decor of glass, wood and aluminium. It is all very sophisticated, tempered and business-like, probably appropriate to Nykredit's status as one of Scandinavia's major financial institutions. Reflecting on this, Kim Holst Jensen says: "Nykredit is a serious organization, and this is a serious building. But it's a light sort of seriousness, with lots of light, views and angles."

One of the two atria in the Nykredit office. All floors are open to the atrium, except for the top floor where the canteen is located. Noise transmission is mitigated by sound-absorbing cladding on all sides of the atrium. The canteen is shielded from the atrium by glazed panels.

Open office at Nykredit. Typical Danish elements: groupings of four desks interspersed with filing cabinets, wood floors, clean design, lots of daylight and Arne Jacobsen furniture.

Open-plan work floors in McKinsey's Hong Kong office. It took some convincing on OMA's part to get the McKinsey partners to shift from a traditional cellular office to a more open and transparent environment.

MCKINSEY, HONG KONG

User: McKinsey
Industry: consultancy
Design: OMA
Location: Hong Kong, China
Size: 1,432 sq.m./ 15,414 sq.ft.
Completion: 2011

It was only to be expected that McKinsey would ask the Office for
Metropolitan Architecture (better known as OMA) to design its Hong
Kong office. Both companies are considered leaders in their field and
they had already worked together on a number of occasions. However,
that was not the main reason for choosing OMA, according to David
Gianotten, the OMA partner in charge of the project: "They wanted
us because of our critical approach to design. We are not afraid to
challenge conventions and ask difficult questions." This was important
to Joe Ngai, the young managing director of McKinsey Hong Kong,
because he was looking for change. He needed a design team that could
challenge McKinsey's brainy, but also rather conservative staff, and
shake up the company's office culture.

The existing McKinsey office had a traditional set-up with large offices
for partners and small open workspaces for the rest of the staff. One
of the first things David Gianotten did was to interview the partners
at McKinsey about how they used their offices. "It quickly became
apparent that many of them are only in the office four or five times a
month. They spend most of their time visiting clients and travelling.
In contrast, their assistants spend long hours in the office, working in
small workspaces with little daylight. Clearly, this was not a smart way
of using the square metres, especially not in Hong Kong where space is
incredibly expensive."

OMA's idea was to invert this model, providing more spacious, day-lit
workspaces for the general staff, and smaller, flexibly used rooms
for the partners. Gianotten knew, however, that this might be a 'hard
sell' for some of the partners. "We decided to present the idea at a
plenary session with everybody there: senior partners, junior partners,
assistants, canteen ladies. As we had hoped, a discussion emerged

and attitudes started to change. Slowly, more and more people became engaged in the design process, forwarding ideas for changes in the office set-up."

Eventually, some of the partners still got their own private offices, but these are smaller than they used to be. The majority of the partner offices are now multifunctional spaces, doubling as team spaces when partners are out of the office. Furthermore, a large part of the office has become open-plan workspace, with flexible desks for travelling staff. Flexibility was added by designing the canteen in such a way that it can provide 25 extra workplaces for McKinsey's 'home Fridays' when all consultants are in house.

To deal with the acoustics of the open plan, ceilings were covered with sound-absorbing materials. Four circular glass telephone booths were created where noisy calls could be made away from the work floor. The booths glow either orange or red, depending on whether or not they are in use.

Comparing the McKinsey office to other OMA projects, it could be argued that the project is rather modest in its expression. OMA's usual wit and irony is visible in certain features, such as the glowing telephone booths, but the overall design is subtle and nuanced. That may be atypical for OMA, but it makes the project fit-for-purpose. McKinsey is a corporate firm. Its dark-suited, busy staff is serious and professional. Too radical an office could have clashed with the identity of the company.

A recent project evaluation revealed that the large majority of the staff are satisfied with their new work environment, says David Gianotten. McKinsey's Beijing office will soon be redesigned according to the same concept, again by OMA. David Gianotten hopes to emulate the success of the Hong Kong project, but he adds: "Do not expect the same design. It is the approach that counts."

Circular phone booths in McKinsey's Hong Kong office. The glazed booths provide space for phone calls, removed from the open plan. The booths glow red or orange, letting staff know when a booth is available.

Open-plan office at McKinsey Hong Kong. The exposed ceiling and epoxy flooring give this otherwise rather corporate office environment the feel of a studio. The wooden desks are custom-made and designed by OMA.

Corridor spaces that connect the various parts of the vast building. These are places where employees can have informal chats, take short breaks or take a private call on their mobile phone.

TAIKANG LIFE, BEIJING

User: Taikang Life
Industry: insurance
Design: Henn Architects with CABR (China Academy of Building Research)
Location: Beijing, China
Size: 70,000 sq.m./ 753,474 sq.ft.
Completion: 2013

With over 54 million clients, Taikang Life is one of the largest insurance companies in China. It is a fully private company that was founded in 1996 in the slipstream of Deng Xiaoping's economic reforms. Since then, Taikang Life has been growing at a double digit rate, actively responding to the insurance demands of China's growing middle class and ageing population.

Taikang Life has an extensive network of retail offices throughout China, but its central operations are based in Beijing. Over the years, multiple offices were leased and acquired to accommodate the company's growth. This led to a situation where business functions were scattered over different buildings and locations. To allow for more efficient communication—and to cut down on real estate costs—the company decided to build a new office complex on the outskirts of Beijing. It currently houses the company's research and data centre, and will soon be extended to accommodate the company's headquarters and a corporate museum.

Architect Wei Sun has been in charge of the project. Wei Sun has worked in various architecture firms in Europe and is now heading the China office of the German firm Henn Architects. When asked to compare office design in Germany and China, Wei remarks that the Chinese office market is maturing. In the past, design quality was often sacrificed to speed of construction, but this attitude is now changing. Wei Sun: "The quality of new Chinese office buildings is rapidly approaching German standards. Clients are getting more demanding and there is increasing awareness of the importance of providing staff with well-designed work environments."

The new office for Taikang Life is a good example of this change in attitude. It is a carefully designed office complex, set in an expansive business park outside Beijing. With a surface area in excess of 70,000 square metres, the building is a vast structure. Yet in many ways it is also a modest building. In contrast to the showy high-rises that are going up in the centre of Beijing, the Taikang Life complex is a rather humble 'ground-scraper' of no more than four storeys. The building is made up of basic rectangular shapes and enclosed by a facade of stone tiles and glass. Wei Sun explains: "The client wanted a low profile building, built with simple, but high-standard means of construction. Furthermore, they wanted the building to express confidence, balance, security and stability, which are important values for an insurance company."

The interior design of the building is governed by principles of openness, transparency and efficiency. Wei Sun: "The people who visit the building should get to see the work processes of Taikang Life and the staff should feel part of the bigger whole." Work floors are mostly open, mixed with cellular offices for management. Wei Sun: "Open-plan offices and cubicles are as popular here as anywhere else. Developers like it because flexible, open spaces are easier to rent out. For occupants it is an efficient solution that allows high densities of workstations." Wei Sun notes that in China workplace densities are generally higher than in Europe, offering relatively little personal privacy. Only management tends to have the luxury of private offices. "Hierarchy is important in China. Managers want to have their own room, which translates into a relatively high demand for single offices."

Space may be tight in many Chinese offices, but Wei Sun points out that the general amenities tend to be generous. The Taikang Life building offers all the usual office facilities, such as a huge canteen and large numbers of conference rooms, but in addition there is also a basketball court, a gym, a library, a café point, and a gathering space for 'cheer-up meetings'. After the company's move-in, several more facilities were added, including a table tennis room and an art gallery. The latter is probably no coincidence as the founder of Taikang Life is the driving force behind China's largest art auction house. Wei Sun: "All these facilities make the office interesting and liveable. The building has become much more than just an office building. I also like the fact that these facilities were added by the company itself. It means the building is interacting with the people who use it. For me, that is one of the top goals of design."

Entrance of the Taikang Life building. A large shiny atrium provides access to the Taikang Life office. The space is also used for large gatherings and speeches by the CEO.

Office interior at Taikang Life. Most workspaces are open, interspersed with various types of meeting rooms. The colour palette is neutral, with lots of whites and greys.

Type 8:
PROCESS OFFICES

Process offices are offices designed for 'low-end' knowledge work, such as data processing or customer services. They tend to be no-frills buildings, filled with cheap cubicles—their design driven by cost efficiency more than anything else. But the character of such workplaces is changing. As routine work processes are being taken over by computers, the remaining work becomes more complex, requiring better skilled workers and better work environments. Some companies do away with offices altogether and outsource their process activities via the Internet to home-based workers.

Publications about workplace design, like this one, tend to focus on workplaces that are visually appealing and designed to accommodate high-end knowledge workers. The imagery features software developers playing video games in their offices, hipster entrepreneurs sipping lattes in cool co-work spaces, and progressive managers holding Skype meetings from the kitchen table in their home. But obviously this is not the reality for all, or even most, office workers. For large groups of 'low-end' office workers, the office is less photogenic, with drab interiors, cheap desks and chairs, dense work floors, noisy air conditioning systems, insipid coffee from vending machines, and long daily commutes.

The biggest contrast is found in process offices like call centres and 'data entry farms', where large numbers of people perform information processing work in a semi-industrial fashion. These work environments tend to be little more than workstation containers, located on cheap sites, designed for efficiency, and devoid of extras or any architectural ambitions. Inside, there are vast open spaces filled with cubicles. Just like the work itself, the interior design tends to be highly standardized and repetitive. Typically, the allocated space per workplace is less than half that of a conventional office.[102]

The origins of this type of office lie in the late 19th century, when the American engineer Frederic Taylor formulated his principles of 'scientific management'. These principles were all about standardization, rationalization and efficiency. They were first applied to factory work, but soon Taylor's followers (known as 'efficiency men') applied them to office work as well. This resulted in a semi-industrial model of the office as a 'white collar factory'. In terms of design, it meant open-plan offices, furnished with lines of desks topped with typewriters.[103] Compared to the traditional offices of that time, the openness allowed better light and ventilation and an uninterrupted flow of work. [104] Just as important was the fact that it created visual overview for managers. The general idea was that people should be closely supervised and pushed to be productive. In keeping with the factory analogy, some offices even featured conveyer belts for transporting paper from desk to desk.[105]

Today, much of the work that was done in the 19th century factory office has been automated. Most of the clerical professions of that era (typists, log-in clerks, validation clerks, stenographers and so on) have been superseded by computers. But this has not resulted in the complete disappearance of low-end office work. Some back-office activities, such as payroll management and other financial administrative tasks are still with us. Furthermore, there are large numbers of people working in call centres (these days also referred to as 'customer interaction centres' and 'contact centres') where they are engaged in providing customer service, selling goods, making or answering inquiries, or in providing technical support—often according to strict procedures and scripts. In addition, new types of routine jobs have emerged. The rise of the Internet has led to a host of new tasks, such as tagging images, editing product databases, writing product reviews, search engine optimization, website testing and so called web content services, such as sifting through social media content to keep websites free from porn and aggression.

Many companies outsource such tasks to specialized companies. The appropriate term for this is 'BPO', which stands for business process outsourcing. Originally, this concept was associated with the outsourcing of manufacturing activities to cheap labour countries, but nowadays outsourcing is also common for office work. In low-wage

Engraving of a telegraph hall in New York, 1860. An image from a different century, yet still very recognizable for those working in call centres today.

countries like India and the Philippines there are entire business districts filled with companies performing outsourced office work for companies in the US and Europe.

It is a trend that is very much related to technological advances. Without powerful Internet connections it would not have been possible to deliver services from low-costs countries to the US or Europe in real time. The work processes themselves are also very much technology-dependent. In contact centres for example, sophisticated software is used to assign and analyse incoming calls, mails and chats, and to monitor performance. In that sense, process work is a highly advanced and very contemporary phenomenon.

In terms of workplace design, however, process offices have not evolved very far from the 19th-century concept of a white collar factory. A pop culture depiction of such an environment can be seen in the award-winning movie *SlumDog Millionaire*, in which the main character works as a tea boy in a call centre in India. The movie's script describes the call centre as "... a room you could swing a Boeing in. Rows and rows of operators in tiny booths stretch into the distance ... Slogans hang from the ceiling. 'When the sun comes up, you'd better be running',

Call centre in New Delhi, 2008. In this Indian call centre, young Indians work as remote debt collectors, making calls to people with payment problems in the United States.

'You snooze, you lose', 'Upgrade for a better, faster life', 'Every call is a new opportunity'."[106]

In critical reviews, process offices are often compared to sweatshops, battery farms and even Roman slave galleons.[107] This is not without reason: labour contracts tend be short-term, wages are low, productivity is measured by means of digital surveillance methods, and the work itself can be very demanding. Typically, staff spend long hours at their workstations, staring almost uninterruptedly at a computer screen. In the case of call centres, people have to take call after call, trying to sell things to unwilling people, or dealing with queries from—often irate—customers "without losing their cool".[108] Not surprisingly, process work is associated with high levels of staff turnover and office ailments such as aching backs, neck and wrists.[109] But the character of process work is changing. Repetitive and rule-based tasks are being automated, resulting in a shift from routine tasks towards more complex types of work, such as resolving technical problems, answering complex non-routine questions and addressing open-ended enquiries.[110] Contact centres are becoming more important because traditional face-to-face contact between

Zappos office, 2008. At the online fashion retailer Zappos, staff are encouraged to decorate their desks. The idea is to promote staff satisfaction and a sense of belonging. (Photo: Shashi Bellamkonda, blog.networksolutions.com)

companies and their clients is decreasing. For banks, for example, the majority of customer interactions no longer take place over the counter in local branches, but over the Internet, via chat, email or phone calls. Such customer contacts have long been seen as 'back office' functions, but they have become the company's 'front office' and have a big impact on how customers perceive a company.

These trends have led to a demand for higher skilled people and more attention to working conditions. The three contact centres that feature in this book (see following pages) are all good examples of this trend. In each project, the attraction and retention of staff were explicitly mentioned as objectives, which translated into the provision of pleasant break areas, ergonomic furniture, training rooms and attractive design. Another interesting example is the call centre of Zappos.com, an online fashion retailer which is much admired for the quality of its service. The work floors at Zappos are as dense and crowded as in other call centres, but the messy and creative atmosphere is a far cry from the Taylorist obsession with neatness and order. At Zappos, all workplaces are personal and staff are encouraged to decorate their desks, providing room for individuality and humour

CTrip call centre. A large part of CTrip's staff works from home, but there are also employees who prefer to work in the office. This is for social reasons or because they find it difficult to work at home, for example when they still live with their parents and don't have sufficient space.

at work. One of the company's core values is 'Create Fun and A Little Weirdness'.[111]

To an increasing extent, process work is also being done from people's homes. Compared to other types of more complex office work, it is relatively easy to allow process workers to work from home because much of the work is individual and staff performance can easily be track digitally (for example, by counting the number of answered phone calls, email response times and customer satisfaction ratings). A well-documented example of this trend is CTrip, China's biggest travel agency. In 2012, CTrip did a telework experiment which was evaluated by researchers from Stanford University. In the experiment, 250 employees were randomly assigned to work from home or in the office for a period of nine months. Detailed tracking of their activities showed that working from home led to a 13% increase in performance, some 9% of which was due to working more minutes per shift (fewer breaks and sick-days) and 4% to making more calls per minute (attributed to a quieter working environment).[112]

Some call centre companies are doing away with their offices altogether. They operate as 'virtual contact centres' or 'cloud contact

Woman working from home for Sykes Home. Sykes Home is a 'virtual call centre'. The benefits for the staff are flexible hours and not having to commute. For the call centre the benefits are savings on equipment and space in combination with higher retention rates.

centres', with all their staff working from home. The advantages are clear: it eliminates the real estate costs and provides lots of flexibility. Moreover, it helps these companies to tap into new labour sources, such as retirees, work-at-home mothers and people with disabilities. One of the largest players in this field is the American company Sykes Home. Using sophisticated software, Sykes Home transfers and reroutes calls, chat sessions and email communication to its staff, who are scattered across over a thousand cities in the US. The company claims that it helps them to deliver better service because they can attract people who are older, better educated, more stable and thus able to handle longer, more complex interactions with customers. The company's website states: "Having a satisfying job doesn't require you to sit for hours in bumper-to-bumper traffic only to spend the rest of the day in a small, dreary cubicle."[113] The company also mentions, however, that working from home comes with certain requirements. Noise in particular is seen as an issue: "In order to maintain a professional environment for our clients ... we recommend your office be behind a closed door. If your children need supervision, you will need to have the proper care set up just like if you were working outside the home. We have a zero-tolerance noise policy."[114]

A step beyond allowing a permanent workforce to work from home is the trend towards 'micro sourcing' or 'crowd sourcing', in which workers are not employed by a company, but contracted on a task-by-task basis via web-based platforms. Amazon's Mechanical Turk was one of the earliest of such platforms, starting in 2005. It is basically a marketplace where companies can post tasks that they want to be performed and individuals can then browse those tasks and select and complete them for a small fee. Tasks are typically small and easy, such as data entry, ranking websites or labelling images. There are now hundreds of such platforms for online labour exchange across the world, and many of them, such Freelancer and oDesk, also broker more complicated tasks such as translations, software testing and programming.

For organizations, the advantage of crowd sourcing is that it can be quick, flexible and cheap. The disadvantage is that it provides less scope for quality assurance, training and control. There are also fewer possibilities for knowledge sharing between the people who perform these tasks. It is quite likely, however, that this web-based model will replace a significant part of the routine work that traditionally goes on in process offices. The consultancy company Accenture argues that today's employers should think of their workforce as made up not just of current full-time employees but also of the vast army of potential workers who are just 'a click away'.[115] In the latter case, work is fully web-based, outsourced, dispersed across the world—rendering the traditional process office obsolete.

Corridor in CBA's customer service centre. Graffiti-graphics give this call centre an 'urban' feel in tune with the relatively young age of the people working there.

CUSTOMER SERVICE CENTRE CBA, MELBOURNE

User: Commonwealth Bank of Australia
Industry: financial services
Design: Davenport Campbell (architecture) and Frost* Design (graphics)
Location: Melbourne, Australia
Size: 11,000 sq.m. / 118,403 sq.ft.
Completion: 2013

Call centres generally do not make exciting examples of workplace design, but the call centre of the Commonwealth Bank of Australia (CBA) in Melbourne is different. This call centre is bright, colourful and vibrant. The design is the result of a collaboration between the architecture firm Davenport Campbell and the design studio Frost* Design. Another important contributor was the New York-based illustrator James Gulliver Hancock. Hancock adorned all seven floors of the CBA office with graffiti-like murals depicting scenes of Melbourne's urban culture, with ghetto blasters, skaters, familiar local buildings, musical instruments—all of it drawn in a psychedelic, comic-like style that is likely to appeal to the relatively young staff of the call centre. But it is not only the graphics that make this call centre exceptional. Just as important is its spatial set-up, which is very different from the 'rack-and stack' layout of traditional call centres. Instead of the usual rows of small, individual cubicles, there is a diversity of team-based desk configurations. Circulation areas are generous and there are a multitude of break areas and informal meeting spaces. On the ground floor there is an advanced staff training centre where staff are taught the finer points of financial service provision. A large open stair case connects all seven floors. Hub cafés on each floor allow staff to hang out and unwind between shifts.
Interestingly, the design of the call centre is quite similar to the bank's new headquarters in Sydney. Both buildings put an emphasis on collaborative spaces, have the same fresh look and feel, and even feature some of the same designer furniture. Architect Neill Johansson

was involved in both projects and explains that these similarities are by no means a coincidence: "The bank deliberately chose to invest in a high quality work environment for its customer services staff. They don't want to differentiate in workplace quality between departments. Their idea is that all of their staff, from top management to call centre agents, should be able to work in an attractive and collaborative environment." Another explanation for the high quality design lies in the increasing importance of customer service centres in retail banking. Traditionally, bank customers would go to their local branch for service. Now, most contact is conducted by phone, email, chat or even videoconferencing. As such, customer service centres play a critical role in shaping customer experience and, ultimately, customer loyalty. Furthermore, the character of the work is changing from handling routine phone calls to more complex interactions in which customers receive advice about the bank's financial products. This means that the staff need to be qualified and talented, expert in both sales techniques and financial products.

All this makes the design of customer service centres more important. Neill Johansson explains: "It is part of CBA's strategy to aim for excellent customer services, so it is only logical that they want to create excellent working conditions for their staff. This means basic things like good chairs and a healthy indoor climate, but in this case it also translated into vibrant and very contemporary aesthetics." The key idea is that good design results in better service and that helps the bank to attract and retain staff. Johansson: "Call centre design is no longer just about 'sweating' the building. It is just as much about enhancing business performance and creating an exciting place to work."

Meeting area in CBA's customer service centre. In addition to workstations, the office also provides generous circulation space and various types of break-out spaces and meeting rooms.

Workspace in CBA's customer service centre. The office provides various types of workstations in different configurations. The classic rows of cubicles are absent here.

Break area in the Banco Santander call centre. The break areas are situated next to light wells that bring daylight into the very large floor plates.

BANCO SANTANDER, QUERÉTARO

User: Banco Santander
Industry: financial services
Design: Estudio Lamela
Location: Querétaro, Mexico
Size: 93,600 sq.m. / 1,007,502 sq.ft.
Completion: 2008

The locals call it the UFO. Banco Santander's call centre in Querétaro is a shiny, circular building that seems to float above its arid, industrial surroundings. Estudio Lamela's Carlos Gomez was the lead architect for the project. He smilingly admits that the nickname is apt. He explains that the building consists of two main volumes: a heavy base, containing all the support functions, and a floating volume of office floors. "We deliberately wanted the office floors to be futuristic and a total contrast to the surroundings. It is an expression of the building's function. The people working here make phone calls to the whole world. The work is 24/7, high-tech, global. It is like a terminal. The local context is irrelevant to this type of work."

The building's size and capacity are impressive. A total of 93,600 square metres (1,007,502 sq.ft.) provides room for over 2,300 workstations. There are 5,200 phone lines that can handle up to 95,000 calls. Phone calls go out to the whole of Latin America, the US and Spain. According to the bank, the centre can securely execute 337,500 transactions an hour.

Banco Santander's design brief explicitly stated that the building was to be the best call centre in the world. This ambition is reflected in the building's iconic design, the advanced cooling system, the sophistication of the IT technologies, and the investment level this entailed. Carlos remarks: "It was great to work with a client with ambition. It has resulted in a high quality building, very different from the cheap call centres that can be seen elsewhere. At Santander, they now joke that the call centre is of better quality than the headquarters office."

To make sure that the building would be productive, the architects wanted to get a good understanding of the nature of call centre work. Carlos: "We interviewed staff members and we quickly learned that working in contact centre can be quite stressful. Call centre agents are calling people who often don't want to be called. It is difficult work. One call after the other, forty to fifty minutes at a stretch, and then a ten minute break." In response, Carlos Gomes and his team did their best to create a calm environment with attractive break areas around large light wells, which act as natural retreats—"places where you can feel the wind and the sun on your skin," as Carlos puts it.

Acoustics were a key consideration in the design process. Specialized consultants were brought in to look at the technical design and conduct simulations of sound levels. Large numbers of acoustic ceiling tiles were used for sound absorption, and it works. On each floor there are more than a thousand people talking into headsets. Yet there is no sense of noise. Individual conversations merge into a soft background murmur. The call centre agents do not have to raise their voices or strain their hearing to communicate with the bank's customers—qualities that are critical for both the well-being and the performance of the staff.

A distinctive feature of the project is its all-grey colour palette. Grey concrete, grey aluminium, grey carpet tiles, grey workstations. The only colour accents come from the furniture in the break areas. Carlos explains: "The grey colour was a wish from the bank. It is one of their corporate colours. I would have liked to add more colour, but I have to say that I like the neutrality and calmness of grey. It is cool, a nice contrast to the blistering heat outside. It is like working in the shade." The building seems to have become the success it was intended to be. According to the bank, staff retention levels have risen significantly since the move-in. Whereas most of the workers were only part-time before, now many of them are working full-time in the call centre. They seem to be glad that the UFO has landed in Querétaro.

Cubicles for managers in the Banco Santander contact centre. Managers get a bit more privacy than the call centre agents. They also have two guest's chairs in their cubicle for small meetings.

Work area in the Banco Santander contact centre. Acoustic panels reduce the sound of over thousand phone conversations to a soft murmur.

Work area in Teletech's call centre. This part of the work area is located in the building's original offices. For budgetary reasons, MVRDV decided to leave the space largely untouched; the floor, lighting and ceiling panels were kept as they were. Teletech added orange parasols to cheer the space up.

TELETECH, DIJON

User: Teletech International
Industry: BPO (business process outsourcing)
Design: MVRDV
Location: Dijon, France
Size: 6,000 sq.m. / 64,583 sq.ft.
Completion: 2012

Teletech's new call centre in Dijon is not a call centre—at least not according to Teletech's CEO Emmanuel Mignot. He prefers to refer to the building as a campus, which is perhaps not so strange since the building is populated by young people, many of them students. They work there part-time and also use the building for 'extracurricular' activities such as studying and starting up their own business. In line with the idea of a campus, almost a quarter of the building's floor area is dedicated to non-call-centre functions such as an education centre, a fitness centre, a gallery and a project incubator.

Jan Knikker is the head of business development of the Dutch architecture firm MVRDV that was responsible for the design of the project. He explains: "The call centre's rush hours are mornings, lunch time and early evenings. In between, activity is low, but for Teletech it is desirable that staff stay in the building, making their operation more flexible." Moreover, Teletech wanted to create an environment that would help them to attract and retain qualified people. Knikker: "Teletech is aware that call centre work generally has a bad image. This project is intended to help to change that, showing that a call centre can also be a creative environment for the staff."

The Teletech call centre is housed in a former mustard laboratory, which had been built for the local Amora mustard brand in 2004. The city of Dijon is famous for its mustards, but the industry is in decline. The Amora laboratory was closed only a few years after its completion because Unilever—Amora's mother company—decided to consolidate its activities elsewhere in France.

When Teletech took over the building, it was almost brand new, but it needed to be adapted. Teletech hired MVRDV for this job, which might be seen as a surprising choice because MVRDV is a highly acclaimed, world famous architecture firm—not really an obvious candidate for a low-budget call centre in Dijon. The story is that Teletech's CEO asked his children which architects they considered 'cool', and MVRDV was on the list.

MVRDV proved to be interested in the project, despite the extremely low budget. Jan Knikker explains: "We are never shy of a challenge and we regarded it as a very relevant project. All over Europe, buildings are empty because of the crisis. As architects, we have to think about how these can be put to new use. It is easy to adapt a beautiful old brick factory close to a city centre. More difficult are cases like this: an unremarkable building, on a fringe location, and hardly any budget. Basically, it was an experiment to see what was possible."

The design strategy was to re-use as many of the building's existing features as possible. It helped that the building was designed as a laboratory, which meant high ceilings and technical services with lots of capacity. In some spaces, MVRDV did little more than remove the existing paint, laying bare the original concrete. In contrast, the canteen was rejuvenated by painting it top-to-bottom in bright orange. In the building's main space, MVRDV created a terraced work floor from basic wooden planks.

The budget limitations did not stop MVRDV from turning the building into an attractive, albeit somewhat 'raw' work environment. The building offers a diversity of work settings, desks come in various configurations, and there are bright orange 'pouffes' (bean bags) the staff can sink into with their laptops. The inspiration for this informal type of work environment came from Teletech's CEO who had noticed that his son hardly ever used his desk for his homework, preferring to sit on his bed with his laptop on his knees. This observation did not result in a deskless call centre, but it did stimulate Teletech and MVRDV to create a low-budget building that represents a new way of thinking about call centre design.

Canteen in Teletech's call centre. The original canteen was given a makeover by covering it top-to-bottom in bright orange paint.

Terraced work area in Teletech's call centre. The ceiling features large acoustic panels to keep sound levels down.

Type 9:

CELL
OFFICES

The cell office, with its long corridors and rows of rooms, is becoming a rarity in the corporate landscape. Progressive architects and consultants consider it the worst option possible: inefficient, introverted and status-driven. In many ways they are right, but employees tend to be quite happy with it, loving the personal space and privacy it offers. Furthermore, it can be argued that cellular offices are good places for thinking and focus work, which are essential activities in a knowledge economy. Time for a reappraisal?

Edward Hopper's *Office at Night* is probably the world's most famous painting of an office. The canvas shows a 1940s office space occupied by a man in a three-piece suit and a woman who is probably his secretary. It is not clear what is going on. The scene is charged and tense. Are they engaged in some clandestine activity? Is she trying to seduce him? Or is it just another tedious long evening of work? Edward Hopper never explained, but he wrote that the inspiration for the painting came from his many rides on the L-train in New York. Passing New York's office blocks in the evening, he caught glimpses of office interiors that were "so fleeting as to leave fresh and vivid impressions on my mind. My aim was to try to give a sense of an isolated and lonely office interior".[116] Hopper's image of isolation and loneliness is consistent with the contemporary critique of the cellular office. In the eyes of change-minded architects, consultants and managers, cellular offices are places of dread and gloom, with closed rooms and silent corridors. In their view, cellular offices are introverted and inefficient; they see the many walls and doors as obstacles that close people in, thereby hindering collaboration and learning—both of which are highly valued concepts in today's management thinking.

Edward Hopper, Office at Night, 1940. Oil on canvas. 56.4 x 63.8 cm. Collection Walker Art Center, Minneapolis.
Edward Hopper said of the painting: "My aim was to try to give a sense of an isolated and lonely office interior".

The adjective 'cell', or 'cellular', does not help the reputation of this office type. It triggers associations with monasteries filled with silent monks and with prisons filled with locked-in prisoners. Erik Veldhoen, a known Dutch office innovator, makes the latter association in his book *The Art of Working*, in which he states that office workers need to be liberated from the cellular office, which in his view is a "habitat for power games" and a "breeding ground for sexual harassment"—ideas that seem to come straight out of Hopper's painting. Veldhoen also remarks that the cell office "encourages cutting corners" and that it is "perfect for intrigue and manipulation".[117] In other words: the cellular office is the evil office.

Veldhoen is not alone in his criticism of the cellular office, nor is he the first. Robert Propst, the inventor of the cubicle, wrote in 1968 that a certain degree of enclosure is necessary for office workers, but that four-sided enclosure would be "bad for the wide awake and activity-oriented man. He is isolated, insulated and remote. His ability to be part of an organizational family is diminished."[118] Similar views were expressed by the proponents of the *Bürolandschaft* (office landscape) in the mid 1960s. They proposed tearing down all walls and creating large open spaces with the objective of improving staff interaction and creating a more egalitarian work environment. The German office consultant Hans Lorenzen declared that it was "really essential that executives should not work in private rooms but in the same room as all the others to create a feeling of all belonging together".[119] A more recent example comes from a 2013 British government guide to 'smart working' which states that "wherever possible, private offices should be removed", noting that these are "very wasteful of space" and that they "can hinder good collaborative working practices."[120]

The fervour of this antipathy is surprising (how bad can a private office really be?), but the critics of the cellular office do have a point. Cellular offices generally do not make for very lively or energetic work environments. Typical layouts consist of long, linear hallways with rows of rooms on either side. When traversing the often labyrinthine corridors one is not really sure whether there are people present inside the rooms, or what these people are doing—although this changes when glazed partitions are used. Furthermore, cellular offices tend to be inefficient. Putting up hard walls and doors is costly and they are not easy to move once they have been installed. Individual offices tend to be more space consuming than open-plan layouts. These inefficiencies are compounded by the fact that the occupants usually spend much of their time outside of their rooms: in meetings, at home, with clients, in classrooms, et cetera.

The difficulty is, however, that office workers tend to be quite happy in cellular offices. There are plenty of studies showing high satisfaction levels for office workers in cellular offices. [121, 122] There is even research that suggests that people who occupy cellular offices are more healthy—less often sick—than workers in open-plan offices. [123, 124]

One of chief merits of cellular offices concerns the personal space and privacy they offer their occupants, shielding them from the sounds, smells, gestures and germs of their co-workers. Another key quality of the cellular office is the relatively high degree of control people have over their work environment. Unlike their counterparts in open-plan offices, they are able to open a window, close the door, adjust the heating or cooling, and possibly even decorate the space—all without having to take the preferences of others into consideration.

These facts and considerations have not had much impact on contemporary office design. According to a 2010 survey conducted

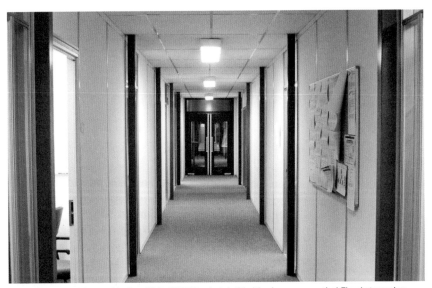

Photo of an empty office corridor from Flickr, 2006. The photo is titled 'business perspective'. The photographer added the following note: "I work here. Pity me ..." (Photo: (a)artwork / Flickr).

by the International Facility Management Association (IFMA), around 70% of office workplaces in the US are open-plan offices (defined as workstations with no partitions or low partitions).[125] There are no such figures available for the rest of the world, but open-plan offices seem to have become the preferred model everywhere. Even in Scandinavia, where small individual offices have for long been the norm for all employees, there is a strong push for more open and flexible office layouts.

There are a few professions and industries where the cellular office still prevails, the most notable examples being the legal sector and academia. Although these sectors, too, are under growing pressure to 'modernize', many lawyers and researchers still work in private offices. It is what they are used to, what they prefer and what they expect. A functional explanation for this lies in the individualistic nature of their work and the high levels of autonomy such workers tend to enjoy. Other factors that may play a role are status sensitivity and an aversion to workplace change, favouring tradition over managerial fads. In a LinkedIn discussion about lawyers' offices, the workplace expert Nigel Oseland noted that it takes "a brave property or facilities manager

According to a 2010 IFMA survey, 89% of senior managers are accommodated in private offices. Don Draper would have approved.

to undo this outmoded obligation of providing private offices."[126]
Another group that has, thus far, successfully managed to hold fast to
their secluded workspaces are the higher echelons of management. The
aforementioned IFMA survey indicates that 89% of senior management
and 98% of top management is accommodated in private offices.[127]
Obviously, this is much to the chagrin to all those who regard executive
offices as anachronistic status symbols. According to them, managers
should not be 'hidden' in wastefully spacious offices, but mix with
the masses and be visible and accessible. In its blog, the General
Services Administration (GSA), which is responsible for the US federal
government's offices, alludes to the television series *Mad Men*, in
which executives occupy plush corner offices with liquor cabinets and
sofas. It comments that "At too many organizations ... this outdated
mentality still exists. We cannot afford to run off of this 1960's model of
working."[128]
As the GSA blog indicates, office innovators tend to view cellular offices
as leftovers from bygone era—a product of tradition more than anything
else. That may often be the case, but there are also organizations that
deliberately opt for cellular offices for functional reasons. The New

Private office at Fog Creek Software, New York. At Fog Creek, all project managers and developers get their own
private office, with a sit-stand desk and a view over the city. The company refers to the extra costs of these features
as "the price of developer happiness".

York-based software firm Fog Creek Software is a good example. In contrast to other tech companies (see chapter 4), Fog Creek provides all of its developers, testers and project managers with private offices. On its website, the company explains: "Our promise has always been that every developer gets a private office with a door that closes. Don't want a private office? You get one anyway. If you want camaraderie, you can walk down the hall, put your witticisms on company chat, or store them all up and let fly at lunch."[129] Fog Creek is aware that private offices are relatively expensive, but they consider them a worthwhile investment: "We're also expressing our company culture by how we structure our office, and if that can keep us happy and motivated, plus attract more smart people who share our values, that's very much worth the extra money."[130]

The Fog Creek example contradicts the widespread idea that the core function of workplace design is to foster interaction. Workplace designers like to talk a lot about how offices can help to facilitate teamwork and collaboration—by creating lots of open space and lots of meeting spots. The assumption is that increased staff interaction promotes the exchange of knowledge and thereby the innovation potential of organizations. There is evidence that supports this idea,[131] but it should not be forgotten that innovation also requires thinking, reflection and contemplation. Such solitary activities may best be supported in distraction-free environments where people's 'flow' of thought is not interrupted by the activities of co-workers.

This idea is strongly promoted by the author Susan Cain. In her book *Quiet: the Power of Introverts,* Cain claims that people are not only more productive, but also more creative when they are free of distractions.[132] In other words: thinking "outside the box" may actually require being in one. She also argues that creative people are often introverts who feel more comfortable in quiet environments than in the hustle and bustle of open-plan offices. To prove her point, Cain quotes a host of well-known creatives and geniuses, including the co-founder of Apple, Steve Wozniak, who said, "Most inventors and engineers I have met are like me—they're shy and they live in their heads. ...They work best when they are alone."

Susan Cain's book provides fresh input to the decades-old debate about open versus enclosed offices. But finding the truth in this debate is difficult. Cain's argument may be valid, but not every office worker is an introverted genius. Most office workers do rather humdrum office work and they operate within teams and departments. Disruptions can be annoying, but for the majority of office workers they are also simply part of their work—a logical side effect of working together with other people. For example, overhearing a phone call or conversation may disrupt one's work flow, but it may also help one to be aware of what is going on, and alert people to the need to offer help and expertise to a co-worker, thereby raising the group's collective productivity.

Workplace research has thus far been unable to settle the debate about cellular versus open-plan offices. There are lots of studies that indicate that—when asked—many people declare a preference for enclosed spaces over open-plan offices. But actual proof that one solution is better than the other is scarce. Most studies rely on self-reported survey data ("how do you rate your productivity?") rather than actual performance data. Moreover, potential organizational effects, such as learning, collaboration, social cohesion and group productivity, tend to be ignored in such studies.

Another issue is that office design does not have a deterministic influence on people's behaviour. Similar office solutions can work out

Shared 'cockpit' at the office of Accenture in Amsterdam. Most new office projects provide a mix of open and enclosed workspaces. So-called quiet rooms and cockpits can be seen as the contemporary interpretation of the cellular office: small, glazed and shared.

differently in different contexts. Cellular offices tend to offer a lot of privacy, but they can also be full of interruptions, with colleagues walking in an out, and people in the room next door making loud phone calls with their doors open. Likewise, open-plan offices are often noisy, but they can also be awfully quiet, to the point where people feel inhibited from talking to one another.[133] This makes it difficult to reach hard conclusions about how office solutions affect organizational behaviour and performance.

Whatever the truth about cellular and open-plan offices, it is not very likely that the traditional cellular office will ever make a grand comeback in contemporary office design. Erecting large numbers of walls and doors has become too expensive and too inefficient by today's standards—especially given that cellular offices stand empty most of the time. Another, perhaps even more important, obstacle is the fact that the cellular office is simply not sexy or appealing enough for change-minded decision makers. Its introverted and closed nature does not sit well with contemporary managerial thinking, which is all about openness, collaboration, knowledge sharing and transparency. The cellular office is widely seen as 'traditional' and 'conventional'—and those are dirty words in today's corporate lexicon.

But pure open-plans are not the answer either. Open-plan offices may help to stimulate collaboration and a more convivial atmosphere, but their disadvantages in terms of noise and distractions are well known. These problems cannot be ignored—especially not in a knowledge economy where thinking is supposed to be a major activity. The obvious solution lies in combining different types of workspace solutions. Many of today's new offices feature open workspaces, but these are mixed with 'focus rooms' and 'quiet zones' where office workers can find peace and quiet. Working from home can also be part of the mix. Most office workers would probably be happy to trade in the luxury of a private office for greater freedom to choose where and when to work. The irony of this last option, however, is that it may leave the office even quieter than if it were a traditional cellular office.

Atrium in the BarentsKrans office. Part of the atrium is used as a library, which has a mainly symbolic function, offering a studious work environment for quiet work.

BARENTSKRANS, THE HAGUE

User: BarentsKrans
Industry: Legal services
Design: Hofman Dujardin Architects
Location: The Hague, the Netherlands
Size: 5,200 sq.m. / 55,972 sq.ft.
Completion: 2013

The lawyers and solicitors of the Dutch firm BarentsKrans have an office that matches the traditions of their business. It is a renovated 1950s building with a monumental marble facade, located on one of The Hague's oldest streets. Inside, the building has two large atria that bring daylight deep into the building, where it is reflected by a shiny travertine floor. On the office floors, the lawyers and solicitors work quietly in spacious office rooms. The materials used are white stucco, glass and light oak. The overall impression is one of quiet sophistication.

The design comes from the firm Hofman Dujardin Architects. Michiel Hofman, the lead designer for the project, explains that the BarentsKrans design brief asked for a contemporary work environment, but that it was clear from the start that BarentsKrans was not looking for something radical or futuristic. "The identity of a legal firm like BarentsKrans is very much about solidity, stability and trustworthiness. The architecture of their offices plays a role in expressing those values. That does not mean that the design should be old-fashioned or boring, but it should not be overly progressive or loud either."

Like many other legal firms, BarentsKrans preferred to have a cellular office layout, with private offices for the partners, two-person rooms for legal staff, and a limited number of open spaces for the support staff. Michiel Hofman would have liked to push for a more open and flexible type of work environment, but that was not really an option here. As he says: "The client's preference for cellular offices has to do with the individual nature of the work and the need for concentration. But it's also a cultural issue. The concept of private offices is deeply ingrained in the culture of the legal industry. It is what staff and partners prefer and expect. Even young lawyers tend to seek the privacy, and status, of a private office. At a certain point this will change, but it takes time."

It is important to point out, however, that the cellular offices at BarentsKrans do not follow the stereotypical image of dark, wood-panelled lawyer's offices where size reflects hierarchy. All rooms have approximately the same size and they are furnished with the same quality of furniture. This standardization is an expression of the relatively egalitarian work culture of the company, but it is also a matter of being practical. Michiel explains: "Same-sized offices make it easier to accommodate organizational change. When people or departments move within the building, there is no need to tear down or replace walls. For the same reason we designed a new type of table that can be used as both meeting table and work table. This made it possible to furnish all rooms in the same way, no matter whether they were one or two-person rooms." A degree of personalization and variety was introduced by allowing staff to choose from a selection of different chairs, lamps and artworks, making every office different while maintaining a large degree of spatial flexibility.

To offset the individual nature of the cellular offices, Michel and his team kept the central parts of the office floors completely open, with pantry facilities and a variety of open meeting spaces. From these floors, the muted sounds of meetings and people chatting at the coffee machine add life to the building's atria.

In the context of the wider discussion about the future of the office, it could be argued that the BarentsKrans office is a rather traditional, or classic, type of office. But it is unlikely that any of the BarentsKrans staff will complain about this. They work in light, airy rooms, with personalized furnishings and doors that can be closed. In this era of flexible working and open-plan offices, these qualities have become rare luxuries.

Open floor in the BarentsKrans office. The open areas with the pantry and meeting spaces form a contrast to the otherwise individual nature of the cellular offices.

Private office at BarentsKrans. A large custom-made table functions as both desk and meeting table. In two-person offices, the same table is used as a work table by both occupants.

Labs and offices in one of the wings of the Bigelow laboratory. The proximity of the offices to the labs was essential, as was the need to have offices for all researchers outside the lab environment.

BIGELOW LABORATORY FOR OCEAN SCIENCES, MAINE

User: Bigelow Laboratory for Ocean Sciences
Industry: research
Design: Perkins + Will / WBRC Engineers
Location: Maine, United States
Size: 5,667 sq.m./61,000 sq.ft.
Completion: 2012

The scientists at the Bigelow Laboratory for Ocean Sciences are literally close to their research topic. Their new building is situated on a coastal hillside in Maine, with uninterrupted views of the Damariscotta River as it flows into the Gulf of Maine. From the building, the scientists can walk down to the Shore Building and dock facility from where they can board research vessels and go out to sea to take measurements and samples. Before the institute moved into the new building, Bigelow's scientists were scattered over seven ageing buildings without proper heating or air-conditioning. The poor quality of the buildings did not stop Bigelow from becoming a world leader in its field, but the working conditions were far from ideal and scientists were cut off from one another.
The objective for the new building was to provide the staff with state-of-the-art lab facilities and to create room for expansion. The building was also expected to help the institute to attract and retain world-class researchers. Funding for the new building came from three key grants, each attached to specific requirements for the building. Together these translated into a research complex with three wings, each dedicated to a specific research area, connected by a 'Commons' building containing meeting rooms and a staff café.
The three wings all have similar layouts: offices on one side, labs on the other, and a hallway in between. The labs are a mix of open and enclosed spaces. The offices consist of private offices for senior scientists and group rooms for junior scientists. It is a classic academic set-up, designed around the idea that researchers—senior researchers in particular—need a place where they can concentrate, think and write. While the cellular set-up allows researchers to work with concentration,

the institute also wanted to promote collaboration. Bigelow prides itself on its cross-disciplinary research and the new building had to enhance this quality. Gary Shaw, the architect from Perkins + Will who was responsible for the architecture of the project, explains: "We tried to create a building that facilitates individual work, but at the same time invites scientists to work together. It is one of the reasons why the offices and labs have fully glazed fronts. This brings in lots of daylight, but it also makes it easy to see one another and to be aware of what is going on." A nice detail is that the glass can be written on. As one researcher noted: "all these writable surfaces make the entire place great for discussion of ideas." Another idea was to promote 'corridor conversations' by widening the hallways and providing whiteboards and pin-up poster spaces along the full length of the hallways.

At the end of each hallway, there is what Gary Shaw calls an 'indoor porch': an open space with a table, chairs and whiteboard space, from where people can enjoy a spectacular view of the shoreline. Gary Shaw: "These spaces are like magnets, bringing the staff together for morning coffee, team meetings, data reviews, or contemplative time developing new research strategies or working on grant applications."

A post-occupancy evaluation of the project showed that the Bigelow researchers are happy with their new building. One of the senior research scientists articulated his satisfaction thus: "This building is way more than a shelter for a group of individual scientists—it's really an instrument to facilitate scientific thought and collaboration across the entire scientific staff."

Glazed wall of one of the Bigelow labs. The writable wall surfaces serve as scratch pads for ideas and explanations.

MiSeq Dilutions

Tube #1: 0.2N NaOH

20 μl 2N NaOH
180 μl H₂O
200 μl

Tube #2: First

2 μl 10nM ØX
3 μl H₂O
5 μl 0.2N NaOH
10 μl

Mix, Spin, 5
Add 990 μl HT1 (hyb buffer)

1 ml @ 20 pM

Tube #2: Final Dilution

675 μl 20 pM ØX
325 μl HT1
1000 μl @ 12.5 pM

→ Loa

Private office at the Bigelow laboratory. It is the office of a senior research scientist at the end of a hallway, adjacent to the 'porch' meeting area.

Private office with a glazed front in the Next World office. The private offices are compact spaces, with just enough room for a workstation, filing cabinet and visitor chair.

NEXT WORLD, SAN FRANCISCO

User: Next World
Industry: Finance
Design: Jensen Architects
Location: San Francisco, United States
Size: 906 sq.m. / 9,750 sq.ft.
Completion: 2013

Next World is an international investment firm, with offices in Brussels, Paris and London, and a head office in San Francisco. The San Francisco office is located in a former print factory in Jackson Square, one of the city's oldest commercial neighbourhoods—which is these days crowded with start-up tech companies and investment firms.
Next World commissioned Jensen Architects to adapt the building to their needs. Frank Merritt was one of the lead architects for the project. He explains that he was rather pleased with Next World's choice of building: "Many of the best qualities of the Next World office are inherent in the existing building: high ceiling, generous skylights and large windowed openings on the street facade. With our architecture, we sought to enhance and celebrate these qualities while weaving-in the client's program."
An important requirement was to include closed workspaces within an open office environment. Some shared space was essential for group meetings and collaborative projects. However, Next World's associates, partners and consultants were all to get private offices. This may seem like a rather conventional choice for such a firm, but according to Frank Merritt it is primarily a functional consideration. He explains that Next World works with sensitive and confidential financial information on a daily basis. Phone calls and meetings about investment possibilities and business deals should be possible without being overheard. Furthermore, the firm's associates and advisors should be able to concentrate when doing their research, making in-depth analyses of business plans and balance sheets, without being disturbed by the sounds of colleagues.
The sensitivity of Next World's work also meant special attention to acoustics. Frank Merritt: "The project required more stringent acoustic

features than the typical office tenant improvement. The challenge was to provide sound separation between the spaces while maintaining natural light and visual openness." This requirement translated into laminated glass panels, gasketed door frames, careful detailing of partitions and stretched-fabric ceilings. Inside the offices, felt panels were used to reduce sound reflection.

Despite the cellular set-up, the Next World office does not make an introverted impression. The private offices are fairly small and they have fully glazed fronts. All the offices are situated around a large 'conversation pit', which is furnished with colourful cushions, a sofa, an oversized purple swing and an informal meeting table. Frank Merritt explains that this sunken space is an artefact of the existing building, perhaps left over from the earlier days when the building served as a cabaret theatre. "We decided to keep this space-defining feature and treat it like a casual living room for use by the users and their guests." A specific request from Next World was to have enough space for their collection of contemporary art. Among various sculptures and paintings, the office features two large murals by local artists: one permanent mural of large colourful flowers, and another wall with a rotating schedule showcasing a new mural every few months.

The resulting atmosphere strikes a balance between the playful style that is typical for the Bay Area's tech companies, and the more restrained expression that is favoured in the financial sector. Frank Merritt notes: "The visible culture at Next World is more business-casual than one might see in other investment companies. The design is rigorous and clearly articulated, but also bright, spacious and welcoming." The welcoming part is interesting because the office is located at street level. With all the glass and openness the workspace is very visible from the entrance doors. Passers-by have already been known to wander in and inquire: Is this a gallery? Is this a restaurant? Or simply: What is this place? Evidently, Jensen Architects has succeeded in creating an office that is far from ordinary.

Private offices in the Next World office. The separations between the different private offices are partly glazed, creating an open atmosphere while maintaining the required acoustic privacy.

Next World's main office area. All the private offices face the 'conversation pit' that is intended for informal meetings and gatherings. Skylights bring natural light into the space.

Type 10:
RECYCLED OFFICES

The traditional model of the office is under pressure as work becomes more flexible, digital and mobile. Could it be that we are, at last, witnessing the demise of the office? It is difficult to say with certainty, but vacancy levels on the office market are shockingly high. Let's just assume that the end of the office is nigh. What then to do with all those empty office buildings? The most productive answer would be 'adaptive re-use', giving tired office buildings a new life as apartments, care facilities, data centres, ateliers or hotels.

In cities across the world, millions and millions of square metres of office space stand empty. According to data from the real estate agency Jones Lang Lasalle, the global vacancy rate for commercial office buildings is around 13 per cent, but in some areas and cities the vacancy rate is as high as 25 per cent or even more.[134] Much of this concerns old, rundown office blocks in unattractive locations, but in some cases even brand new projects in inner cities are having difficulty finding tenants. The reason for all this emptiness is the pairing of economic recession with an overbuilt stock of office buildings. In the past few years, organizations have been downsizing their operations because of economic conditions, while at the same time a flood of new, speculative office development has come onto the market. Seasoned observers of the real estate market say that this mismatch between demand and supply is just temporary and that vacancy levels will go down as soon as economic growth returns. Peter Murray, chairman of London's Centre for the Built Environment, told *The Independent*: "I've seen four recessions during my career—and in each one I've heard people say, 'Look at all this empty office space, why do we need it?' And after each one as the economy has improved, it has become occupied."[135]

Empty office block available for rent in Madrid, 2012. The problem of empty office space is to a large extent created by the current economic crisis, but more fundamental changes, such as the digitalization of office work, are also likely to play a role in the decreasing need for office space.

There is no denying that today's high vacancy levels are caused by economic problems—which may recede at a certain point—but there are also reasons to believe that the demand for office space is undergoing profound change. The most visible impact comes from mobile working and the flexibilization of the labour market. As explained in the first three chapters of this book, today's knowledge workers operate out of many other places besides office buildings. While the office market is weak, there has been a boom in all sorts of co-work spaces and Wi-Fi-powered coffee houses that cater to the needs of nomadic and/or independent knowledge workers. Furthermore, increasing numbers of people work from their kitchen tables and IKEA desks at home—maybe not as many as predicted, but according to the advocates of new ways of working, the tipping point for remote work is near.[136]

With office workers no longer tied to their desks, many organizations are taking a critical look at their space consumption. Noting that much of their office space is underutilized, they are adopting flexible office concepts such 'desk sharing' and 'hotelling', with fewer desks than office workers. In addition, many organizations are opting for open-plan

Squatted office building in Amsterdam 2013. After standing empty for some time, this office building was squatted by a group of local artists and entrepreneurs. Recently, however, the building was sold to a private investor who will transform it into hotel.

office layouts that are highly efficient in their use of space. As a result, the office space per worker ratio is dropping. Research from CoreNet (an international association of real estate professionals) shows that the average amount of space per office worker has decreased significantly in the past few years, going from 21 square metres (225 square feet) in 2010, to 14 square metres (150 square feet) or less in 2013.[137] It is a downward trend that is expected to continue as more organizations adopt flexible office concepts and desk-to-worker ratios are further optimized.

Another development, which may have an ever bigger impact on the demand for office space, is the digitalization of work. As information technologies continue to become more powerful and intelligent, it is likely that major chunks of office work will be taken over by machines. It is the continuation of a decades-long trend. Office buildings in the 1950s and '60s were filled with large numbers of typists and clerks, whose functions no longer exist because they have been automated. The same may happen to many of today's office jobs. The expectation of technology experts is that many of tomorrow's jobs will be performed by advanced robots and digital agents rather than human beings.[138] Research from Oxford University suggests that the bulk of the work done by office and administrative support workers could be automated relatively soon, perhaps over the next decade or two.[139] Routine jobs and rule-based tasks in particular are under pressure: think of the work of data-analysts, financial traders, telemarketers, translators, sales agents, administrators, planners, legal assistants, help desk staff, accountants and technical writers. Jobs that require a high level of creativity or social skills may continue to exist for some time, but the general outlook is not very promising. As a columnist for *The Economist* wrote, "most office jobs will eventually go the way of the dodo."[140]

If the above is true, the future of the office as a building type looks bleak. One doom scenario would see the digitalization of office work turn today's bustling office districts into tertiary wastelands, with desolate parking lots overgrown with weeds, crumbling office buildings covered in graffiti, and empty office floors populated by squatters and stray dogs rather than busy office workers. Such an office apocalypse may seem far off, but it can be argued that similar things have happened before in the industrial sector. During the industrial revolution, many cities were busy places of production, filled with factories and warehouses, their skylines punctured by smoking factory chimneys. In the mid 20th century, all this changed. Production processes were automated and activities were outsourced and moved to cheaper locations, leaving cities with obsolete factories, empty warehouses and decaying industrial areas. Why shouldn't something similar happen to the office sector?

Obviously, the future is fraught with uncertainties. It is not the first time that the end of the office has been proclaimed. In the early 1980s, the futurologist Alvin Toffler foresaw a future in which people would live and work in 'electronic cottages' in the countryside, leaving inner-city office towers "half empty and reduced to use as ghostly warehouses or converted into living space".[141] Thus far, such visions have not become reality. The office has proved to be a rather tenacious phenomenon because of the continuing importance of face-to-face interaction, and perhaps also because of organizational inertia and fear of change. Yet it is crystal clear that work processes and workplaces are changing. Mobile working has become a mainstream phenomenon. New technologies allow people to work anytime and anyplace. Work is being digitalized. More and more people work as freelancers and independent

Cubicles by the Dutch artist Arnout Killian (Oil on canvas, 2011). Arnout Killian made a series of paintings depicting office spaces that are devoid of life. Could it be that these desolate, somewhat sinister scenes depict the future of the office?

workers. The use of office space per employee is falling. So, it is not entirely unthinkable that we are indeed witnessing the demise of the traditional office.

Let's just assume that this is true. It would immediately prompt the question: what to do with all that empty office space, all those huge corporate towers and expansive business parks for which there is no longer a functional need? The most productive answer would be to recycle empty office buildings for new uses, turning them into housing, ateliers, start-up spaces, data centres, hotels, care homes or educational facilities. The appropriate technical term for this is 'adaptive reuse', which is formally defined as "the process of reusing an old site or building for a purpose other than that for which it was built or designed."[142]

Such a recycling approach would be more productive than demolition or decay. From an environmental point of view, there is the advantage of not having to use new materials and avoiding the waste that comes with demolition. It would also make sure that existing infrastructure, such as roads, bus stops, sewage, data and electricity cables, does not go to waste. The socio-economic advantage is that new uses can help to hold

Cover of *The Economist*, January 18, 2014. The Economist argues that a third great wave of invention and economic disruption, triggered by advances in information and communication technology (ICT), will shake up today's work processes.

on to activities and people in areas that would otherwise fall victim to self-perpetuating decay.

Adaptive re-use is no easy solution though. Part of the challenge is technical. Transforming an office building into a hotel or student housing can be hindered by floor plans that are too narrow or too deep, by limited floor-to-ceiling heights and poorly insulated facades. Furthermore, there will be the issues of plumbing, ventilation systems and fire safety. Owing to these technical issues, reuse is sometimes more expensive than demolition and the construction of a new building, although the three examples in this book are examples where construction actually got cheaper and faster because of the re-use of existing structures.

The biggest challenge, however, concerns the location of buildings. The 'triple L' of real estate development—location, location, location—is just as relevant for adaptive reuse as it is for new development. Hilde Remøy, an assistant professor from Delft University of Technology is an expert on the redevelopment of office buildings. She points out that most successful examples of the adaptive reuse of office buildings are inner-city projects. The transformation of buildings in peripheral, mono-

Pop-up hotel by PinkCloud, 2013. The Danish architecture collective PinkCloud produced a proposal for creating pop-up hotels on empty office floors in Manhattan. Real life equivalents of this idea are the Qbic hotels in Amsterdam and London (see page 295).

functional business parks is much harder to realize.[143] Such areas tend to be sited far away from shops, schools and housing and to lack proper public transport. With only other structurally vacant office buildings surrounding them, there is little interest from developers or investors to do anything with these buildings because they see no potential inhabitants.

From this perspective, empty office space seems to be a structural rather than a contingent problem. And yet real estate developers continue to build new office buildings, adding more and more space to the market. The reason for this is that tenants usually prefer new buildings to old ones because they are more efficient, more sustainable, more flexible or located in better areas. So, new buildings go up on favourable locations with rising rent levels, while a vast stock of old, inefficient buildings remains empty. Real estate experts talk of the 'fruit bowl syndrome': the attractive, fresh fruit is being eaten first, while the older fruit is being left to rot.

To deal with this disparity, cities may have to think about limiting new development and considering radical redevelopment plans for old office areas, looking at transport, housing and services. And for seriously 'rotten fruit', demolition is probably the only option. As for new office development, developers, tenants and architects need to think more about flexibility and the future use of buildings. Offices will not cease to exist, but the demand will certainly change. Ideally, new buildings and office locations can adapt to change and allow for different uses over time. In the endgame of the office, adaptability is the key word.

Lecture room at the Rotterdam University. One of the challenges of converting office space into lecture rooms lies in the limited floor-to-ceiling height. Large, steeply raked lecture halls would not have been possible here.

ROTTERDAM UNIVERSITY OF APPLIED SCIENCES, ROTTERDAM

User: Rotterdam University of Applied Sciences
Industry: education
Design: Rogier van den Berg and Daan Zandbelt (building),
Buro M2R (interior)
Location: Rotterdam, the Netherlands
Size: 25,000 sq.m. / 269,097 sq.ft.
Completion: 2011

The Rotterdam University of Applied Sciences has turned an office block
that was destined for vacancy into a vibrant educational facility. The
25,000 square metre (269,097 sq.ft.) building is located on the edge of
Rotterdam's city centre. It is a modernist, bland building, dating from
the late 1980s. For over twenty years, it served as the head office of the
Dutch energy company Eneco, but in 2012 the company decided to move
to a newly built office building on the outskirts of Rotterdam.
For Credit Suisse—the owner of the building—finding a new tenant was
not likely to be easy. As elsewhere in the Netherlands, the local demand
for office space was—and still is—at a record low. The Rotterdam
University of Applied Sciences, however, showed immediate interest in
the building. They already occupied several buildings close by and the
Eneco building fitted their ambition to create a 'city campus' in the area.
An additional benefit was that the building came with ample parking—a
rare luxury in the centre of Rotterdam.
The university got to hear about the building's availability because they
were actively involved in the master planning of the area. This meant
they were able act quickly and start negotiating directly with the owner
of the building before it came on to the market. A major part of the
negotiations concerned the financing of the necessary modifications to
the building, but these negotiations were made easier by the fact that
the university was prepared to lease the building for an extended period.
Broadly speaking, it was agreed that the owner of the building would

invest in structural changes to the building, while the university would pay for the fit-out.

Architects Rogier van den Berg and Daan Zandbelt were brought in by Credit Suisse to make the structural changes to the building. Their main challenge was to ensure that the building would be able to cope with the large numbers of students who would be using the building. Rogier van den Berg explains: "The number of students was going to be much higher than the number of office workers for whom the building was originally designed. This made logistics and fire safety our major concerns. To be able to accommodate the large flows of students, we located all common functions, such as the restaurant and the lecture halls, in the low-rise part of the building, while we positioned staff functions in the tower. Furthermore, we widened corridors and added new elevators and staircases."

In addition to the logistical changes, the architects wanted to make the building more light and open. The building's original interiors were dark, with lots of corridors and small office rooms. All this was stripped out and replaced with a more open and transparent set-up. Furthermore, new glazed facade panels were added to bring more daylight into the building. A new entrance was created to make the building "more permeable to its surroundings," as Van den Berg puts it.

In spite of these major modifications, implementation went very smoothly. Van den Berg: "The total project period, from the start to completion, was just one year. Such speed would not have been possible when constructing a new building of such size. Just think of the site logistics on an inner city location like this. Moreover, putting up a new building would have meant new permits and complying with new zoning and construction regulations. This would made the project more expensive and time-consuming."

In addition to being efficient, Van den Berg argues that the reuse of the building is a sustainable solution because it makes intensive use of an existing structure. "There is less construction waste and a smaller need for new materials." Moreover, there are benefits for the surrounding area. Instead of an empty office block, there is now a vibrant building that is bringing large numbers of students into the area. "It makes the area livelier, safer and it is beneficial for local retailers and food outlets. All this makes the project a good case of adaptive re-use," says Rogier van den Berg. He concludes: "Why build new when there is so much you can reuse?"

Teaching space at Rotterdam University. Most teaching spaces are located on the ground floor to avoid large numbers of students having to travel up and down in the building.

'Learning landscape' at Rotterdam University. This is an area where students can work on their assignments, both individually and in groups. The similarities with contemporary open-plan office layouts are striking.

Café of the Park Theatre. Turning the former office into a theatre helped to bring new life to this street. The theatre attracts people in the evening and the largely open and glazed facade adds to a sense of safety for people passing by.

PARK THEATRE, LONDON

User: Park Theatre
Industry: culture
Design: David Hughes Architects
Location: London, United Kingdom
Size: 1,100 sq.m. / 11,840 sq.ft.
Completion: 2013

Park Theatre is located in a quiet street in Finsbury Park. It is a building of modest scale, squeezed in between other low-rise buildings, but it makes its presence known by way of its red facade, illuminated lettering and the café that edges out of the building's front. It is hard to imagine that this building was once an unassuming office block, where there were office workers working behind desks instead of actors performing on stage and people having drinks in the cafe.

When the founders of Park Theatre discovered the building, it had been standing empty for more than a year. The building's previous user, a charity, had moved out and property developers had little interest in the building because the demand for office space in the area was low and zoning requirements did not allow the building to be converted into residences. The people from Park Theatre, however, saw potential. They had been searching for an appropriate building for six years, and they felt that they had finally found a suitable, affordable home for their theatre.

The prime reason for choosing this particular building was its location. The building is in an unremarkable street, but it is just around the corner from the Finsbury Park underground station. That makes the building only a short ride from the West End—London's main theatre district. Furthermore, there were no other theatres in Finsbury Park, an area that was undergoing a transformation process that was resulting in more and more 'culturally hungry' people coming to live there.

The building itself was of a good size and had a fairly robust structure, which would allow for major adjustments without having to demolish the building. In addition, the building's steel rooftop construction provided an opportunity to create three apartments on top of the theatre. These apartments were a crucial part of the plan because their sale would help to finance the project, which was entirely dependent on private funding. Architect Dave Hughes was responsible for designing the new theatre. His task was to turn the tired office building into a first-rate, friendly and welcoming theatre. The design brief specified two stages, a theatre café, and a host of support spaces such as storage rooms, dressing rooms and a loading area.

Dave Hughes explains that one of the main challenges was the narrowness of the site and the limited height of the office floors. To turn the building into a theatre, he had to cut through floors, raise ceilings and create a new facade. At the same time, he tried to work with the existing structure. Hughes: "We exposed, kept and celebrated as much of the old materials as possible, such as the bare brick, concrete floors and steel construction." He also retained the basic set-up of the building, with a front building, a back building and an atrium in between. According to Hughes, the history and limitations of the building contributed to the eventual success of the project: "An existing building brings its own character and challenges, but by using those you create something much more interesting. The trick is to work with the existing building as much as possible – let it speak to you and lead the design process."

Foyer of the Park Theatre. The adaptive re-use of the building was realized within a very tight budget. The building's finishes are basic and much of the furniture is second-hand.

Atrium of the Park Theatre. Turning an old office building into a theatre calls for major changes and modification of the building's design, but architect David Hughes left as much as possible of the original structure intact.

Hotel room with the Cubi element. The Cubi is an integrated, prefabricated element that combines a bathroom, luxury bed and television set. The element was developed specifically for converting existing buildings into hotels. It can be assembled within a few hours and then just needs to be hooked up to the building's technical services.

QBIC, LONDON

Users: Business travelers, tourists
Industry: hospitality
Design: Qbic, together with Blacksheep
Location: London, United Kingdom
Size: 4,645 sq.m./ 50,000 sq.ft.
Completion: 2013

London's office market is slowly recovering from the financial crisis: demand is picking up, vacancy levels are decreasing, rent levels are rising. Even so, London still has plenty of empty office buildings. These are often outmoded, derelict buildings, outside London's prime business locations. These buildings seem to have little future, even if the office market were to fully recover to pre-crisis conditions. There seem to be only two options: demolition or adaptive re-use. A successful example of the latter is the new Qbic hotel.

The London Qbic hotel is located in a former 1960s office building in the Whitechapel area, which had been standing largely empty for years. Shabby and relatively cheap, the building presented an excellent opportunity for Qbic to establish their first London hotel. The hotel is targeted at business travellers and tourists who seek the comfort and design of boutique hotels, but do not want to pay premium prices. Making use of existing buildings is a key element of Qbic's strategy to keep prices low. Paul Rinkens, one of the founders of Qbic, explains: "Buildings are the most capital intensive and risky part of the hotel business. Why would you put an immense amount of capital and effort into erecting a new building, when there are so many empty buildings available? Using vacant office buildings allows us to keep costs down, and, consequently, to offer sharply priced rooms."

Central to Qbic's way of working is the 'Cubi', which is a patented, aluminium modular unit which integrates a luxury bed, a small workstation, a bath and toilet, lighting, air conditioning and a television. These prefabricated units make it relatively easy to transform office buildings into hotels once you have stripped them. "It is a plug and play approach, with little actual construction work for the fit-out." says Paul. The units are designed in the Netherlands, prefabricated in China and then shipped as flat-packs to the construction site. In a matter of hours, the units are assembled in the otherwise empty rooms. The next step is to hook them up to the building's technical services with flexible ducts for water, waste, electricity and air.

According to Paul, this way of working is both cheaper and faster than traditional hotel construction. He points out that the fit-out of the Qbic hotel in London took six months instead of the usual ten to eleven months. Furthermore, the Cubi concept makes the project more sustainable. Because of the high level of prefabrication, construction waste is minimal and at the end of the hotel's life time, the units can easily be dismantled and recycled or used elsewhere.

Paul Rinkens got the idea for the Cubi unit when he was watching a play in a theatre. "I noticed how the scene was changed two to three times during the play—quickly and effortlessly. It was a total contrast to the slow and static way of operating in the construction industry. It convinced me that we should move away from the fixed and solid solutions. I wanted to create a solution that was flexible, quick and lean."

Despite the many advantages of their approach, the Qbic hotel chain's expansion has proved more difficult than expected. "It is a new way of thinking and that doesn't make it easy to sell," notes Paul. "Our target groups are property developers and real estate owners. We offer them a smart way for making a profit from empty buildings, but the property business is conservative. They want proven concepts."

With the success of Qbic's hotel in London, however, Paul expects his hotel chain to grow more quickly. There are plans for Qbic hotels all over Europe. But his ambitions reach beyond the hotel business. Paul Rinkens believes that Cubi concept can also be used for social housing, student accommodation and even the sheltering of refugees. "I want to do something positive. If you look at the world right now, there are large numbers of refugees and lots of disaster areas. More than ever there is a need for quick and cheap housing. I think the Cubi concept can play a role in meeting that need."

View from one of the hotel's rooms. When Qbic turned the building into a hotel, little had to be done to building's facade, except for changing the windows.

Bench in the foyer of the Qbic hotel. The building is no longer an office, but there is still a lot of office work going on. The power outlets in the bench were specifically made for this purpose. Obviously there is also free Wi-Fi.

EPILOGUE

This book is full of photos of people staring at computer screens—their eyes narrowed, their bodies hunched forward, their minds absorbed by what is on their screen and, one hopes, being very productive. In that sense, the images are all very similar. The settings and backdrops, however, differ widely. There are people working in sunny parks, city squares, moving trains, cosy cafés, hotel lobbies, co-work spaces, even garden sheds. In addition, there examples of all sorts of offices— expansive open-plans, small cubicles, spacious corner offices, shared desks, messy studios, austere modernist offices, and playful offices with slides and surf boards. These are all workplaces, and they are all very different in terms of design, comfort, expression and facilities. This diversity begs the question whether one workplace is better than the other. Is it better to work in a buzzing open-plan or in a quiet private office? At a personal workstation or an anonymous 'hot' desk? In cheerful offices with foosball tables, or in corporate offices with clean desks? Or maybe it is best not to have an office at all?

It is difficult, if not impossible, to answer such questions in absolute terms. The people interviewed for this book—designers, consultants, project managers, facility managers, users—all expressed strong, often opposing opinions on these matters. For example, some were very much in favour of the idea of the flexible office, cherishing the freedom of choice such concepts offer, whereas others saw them as a thinly veiled attempt to save on real estate costs. A similar divergence of views can be found in workplace literature and in the discussions on social media. On LinkedIn and Twitter, the pros and cons of open-plan offices and working from home are fiercely debated.

So, there is no shortage of opinions about workplace design. The difficulty is to find solid evidence to substantiate these opinions. Scientific research provides factual input, but it seldom provides clear-cut answers. There are many interesting studies around—see the reference section of this book—but the outcomes tend to be either very case-specific or very general in nature. It is also not unusual for different studies on similar office concepts to produce divergent, contradictory results. For example, some studies indicate that open-plan offices promote staff interaction, while others suggest quite the opposite.[144]

Why is it so difficult to come up with 'hard truths' about workplace concepts? One reason is that workplace design is just one of the many factors that influence people's behaviour and performance. Workplaces are important, but so are people's motivation, the quality of management, organizational strategies, economic circumstances, the technologies used, and the organizational culture. This jumble of influences makes it difficult to say with certainty how particular workplace solutions affect people and the organizations they work for. Another difficulty lies in the 'low criticality' of workplace design. [145, 146] Office work comes with certain 'critical' needs concerning space (enough space to sit), comfort (not too cold/hot, enough light, not too noisy), and facilities (availability of Wi-Fi and coffee), but once these needs have been met, the notion of workplace quality becomes much more elusive and subject to rather intangible factors such personal preferences, managerial fashion, design trends and cultural norms and values.

The low criticality of workplace design does not mean that it is irrelevant or an entirely subjective matter. It does mean, however, that discussions about workplace design can become very slippery once the basics have been covered. It is fairly easy to discuss the appropriate air quality and temperature levels in an office because these are measurable, well-studied aspects of workplace quality. More conceptual issues, however, such as the openness of workspaces or the freedom to work from home, are much more value-laden and open to debate.

The elusive nature of workplace quality should not discourage workplace designers and decision makers. It just means that they should be willing to engage in an active dialogue with office users in an attempt to create a shared vision of what a good work environment entails. It calls for a 'situational approach' in which the design process is preceded by analysis. Where and how do people work? What type of people are involved? Where do organizational priorities lie? What is the organizational culture like? And how will all this develop in the near future? Answering such questions can provide an understanding of people's work styles, needs and expectations—which is essential input for a successful design process.

As can be seen in this book, the outcome of such process may in many cases still be a classic office building. Four decades after Hans Hollein's invention of the 'mobile office', there is still a strong belief in the synergies that can occur when people work side by side in a physical office space. At the same time, however, it is clear that the office is losing its sense of inevitability as a solution. For decades now, large numbers of people have been working at home, in public spaces, and other 'non-office' places. This trend is likely to continue in the future as work becomes ever more digital and flexible. Whether this will bring down the traditional concept of the office remains to be seen. It seems safe to conclude, however, that today's work environment offers more technological, spatial and organizational possibilities than ever before. The art and science of workplace design is to make optimal use of these possibilities and to create solutions that are efficient, attractive, sustainable and meaningful.

REFERENCES

Introduction

1   Veldhoen, E., & Piepers, B. (1995). *The demise of the office. The digital workplace in a thriving organisation*. 010 Publishers.
2   Miller, P. (2012). *The Digital Workplace: How Technology Is Liberating Work*. Dog Ear Publishing.
3   Lister, K., & Harnish, T. (2009). *Undress for Success: The Naked Truth about Making Money at Home*. John Wiley & Sons.
4   Macrae, N. (1978). How to survive in the age of 'telecommuting'. *Management Review*, 14-19.

Home Offices

5   Rybczynski, W. (1987). *Home: A Short History of an Idea*. Penguin Books.
6   Hawley III, J. C. (2008). *"Spreekt, Schilderij... Swijgt, Schilderij": Some Thoughts on Thomas de Keyser's 1627 Portrait of Constantijn Huygens and His Clerk*. Doctoral dissertation, The College of William and Mary.
7   Nilles, J.M. (1998). *Managing Telework: Strategies for Managing the Virtual Workforce*. Wiley.
8   Nilles, J. M. (1976). *Telecommunications-Transportation Tradeoff: Options for Tomorrow*. John Wiley & Sons, Inc.
9   Ibid
10 Ibid.
11 U.S. Bureau of Labor Statistics (2013). *American time use survey —2012 results*. Available at: www.bls.gov/news.release/pdf/atus.pdf (Accessed: 5 May 2014).
12 Wardman, M., Batley, R., Laird, J., Mackie, P., Fowkes, T., Lyons, G., Bates, J. and Eliasson, J. (2013). *Valuation of travel time savings for business travellers*. Project Report. Department for Transport. Available at: http://eprints.uwe.ac.uk/21950/ (Accessed: 5 May 2014).
13 Paul Carder (@paulcarder), #commutingtoday, *Twitter*. No longer available (Accessed: 6 May 2011).
14 Slijkhuis, J. M. (2012). *A structured approach to the need for structure at work*. University Library Groningen.
15 Johnson, A. (2010). *Shedworking: The Alternative Workplace Revolution*. Frances Lincoln.
16 Dahl, R. (1979). *The Wonderful Story of Henry Sugar and Six More*. Bantham Books.
17 Davenport, T. (2005). 'Why office design matters', *HBS Working Knowledge*. Available at: http://hbswk.hbs.edu/archive/4991.html (Accessed: 5 May 2014).
18 Boell, S., Cecez-Kecmanovic, D., and J. Campbell (2014). Telework and the nature of work: an assessment of different aspects of work and the role of technology. *Proceedings of the 22nd European Conference on Information Systems*, Tel Aviv 2014
19 Swisher, K. (2013). "Physically Together": Here's the Internal Yahoo No-Work-From-Home Memo for Remote Workers and Maybe More. *All things D*. Available at: http://allthingsd.com/20130222/physically-together-heres-the-internal-yahoo-no-work-from-home-memo-which-extends-beyond-remote-workers/ (Accessed: 10 September 2014).

20 Trump, D. (2013). @MarissaMayer is right to expect Yahoo employees to come to the workplace vs. working at home. She is doing a great job!, *Twitter*. 25 February. Available at: https://twitter.com/realDonaldTrump (Accessed: 8 September 2013).
21 Branson, R. (2013). Give people the freedom of where to work. *Richard Branson's blog*. Available at: www.virgin.com/richard-branson/give-people-the-freedom-of-where-to-work (Accessed: 5 May 2014).
22 DeGuzman, G. V., and A. I. Tang (2011). *Working in the Unoffice: A Guide to Co-working for Indie Workers, Small Businesses, and Nonprofits*. Night Owls Press LLC.

Public speces

23 Badger, E. (2012). How Smart Phones Are Turning Our Public Places Into Private Ones. *The Atlantic*, 16 May. Available at: www.citylab.com/tech/2012/05/how-smart-phones-are-turning-our-public-places-private-ones/2017/ (Accessed: 5 May 2014).
24 Parsons, T. (2012). The Outdoor Office, *Domus*, Available at: http://www.domusweb.it/en/design/2012/04/03/the-outdoor-office.html (Accessed: 5 May 2014)
25 Hemingway, E. (2010, first published in 1964), *A Moveable Feast*. Random House.
26 Information Policy and Access Center (2014). *Public libraries& access*. Available at: http://digitalinclusion.umd.edu/sites/default/files/CommunityAccessIssueBrief2014.pdf (Accessed: 25 August 2014)
27 Attlee, J. (2012). About this site. *Writer on the train*, July 12. Available at: http://writeronthetrain.com/ (Accessed: 5 May 2012).
28 Gergen, Kenneth J. (2002). The challenge of absent presence. In: Katz, James E. and Aakhus Mark A.(eds.) *Perpetual Contact. Mobile Communication, Private Talk, Public Performance*. Cambridge University Press, 227-241.
29 Hatuka, T., and Toch, E. (2014). The emergence of portable private-personal territory: Smartphones, social conduct and public spaces. *Urban Studies*, 0042098014524608.
30 Hampton, K. N., Goulet, L. S., and G. Albanesius (2014). Change in the social life of urban public spaces: The rise of mobile phones and women, and the decline of aloneness over 30 years. *Urban Studies*, 1, 16.
31 Whyte, W. H. (1980). *The Social Life of Small Urban Spaces*. Project for Public Spaces Inc.
32 Gregor, A. (2012). Bryant Park Office Rents Outperform the Rest of Midtown. *New York Times*. Available at: http://www.nytimes.com/2012/10/03/realestate/commercial/bryant-park-office-rents-outperform-the-rest-of-midtown-manhattan.html (Accessed: 10 June 2013)
33 Foursquare (2011), Available at: https://foursquare.com/v/ace-hotel-lobby-bar/4adfb640f964a520e57c21e3

Co-work offices

34 Neuberg, B. (2007). *Co-working: 2 Years and Going Strong*. March 11. Available at: http://codinginparadise.org/weblog/2007_03_11_archive.html (Accessed: 17 June 2014).
35 Neuberg, B. (2005). *Co-working – Community for Developers Who Work From Home*. August 9. Available at: http://codinginparadise.org/weblog/2005/08/co-working-community-for-developers-who.html (Accessed: 17 June 2014).
36 Ibid.
37 Ibid.
38 Becker, F. D., and F. Steele (1995). *Workplace by design: Mapping the high-performance workscape*. Jossey-Bass.
39 Frost, D. (2008). 'Co-working,' a cooperative for the modern age. *New York Times*, February 21. Available at: www.nytimes.com/2008/02/21/technology/21iht-co-work.1.10263648.html (Accessed: 18 June 2014).
40 Taddei, A. (1999). *London Clubs in the Late Nineteenth Century*. University of Oxford.
41 Wikipedia (2014). *Co-working*. Available at: http://en.wikipedia.org/wiki/Co-working (Accessed: 17 June 2014).
42 Jackson, K. (2013). *Making Space for Others*. Available at: http://makingspaceforothers.com/content/home/MakingSpaceForOthers_By_Katy_Jackson_sml2.pdf (Accessed: 17 June 2014).
43 Foertsch, C. (2013). *4.5 New Co-working Spaces Per Work Day*. March 4, Available at: www.deskmag.com/en/2500-co-working-spaces-4-5-per-day-741 (Accessed: 17 June 2014).
44 Foertsch, C. (2011). *The Co-worker's Profile*. December 13, Available at: www.deskmag.com/en/the-co-workers-global-co-working-survey-168 (Accessed: 17 June 2014).
45 Millennial branding and ODesk (2013), *Millennials and the Future of Work*, Available at: www.odesk.com/info/spring2013onlineworksurvey/ (Accessed: 17 June 2014).
46 Vos, W. (2013). *London Campus: at the heart of a thriving and diverse startup scene*. Available at: www.campuslondon.com/static/public/pdf/Campus_report_dec_2013_spreads.pdf (Accessed: 17 June 2014).
47 Neuberg, B. (date unknown). *Co-working: Community Office Space for Writers and Programmers*. Available at: http://codinginparadise.org/co-working/ (Accessed: 17 June 2014).

Play offices

48 Stewart, J.B. (2013). A Place to Play for Google Staff. *The New York Times*, 16 March, B1.
49 Newman, R. (2010). 15 Trends That Will Reshape Your Office. *US News*, 22 March. Available at: http://money.usnews.com/money/blogs (Accessed: 5 May 2014).
50 Jacob, S. (2013). Offices designed as fun palaces are fundamentally sinister. *Dezeen*, February 28. Available at: www.dezeen.com/2013/02/28/opinion-sam-jacob-fun-office-design-sinister/ (Accessed: 5 May 2014).

51 Hanley, W. (2012). Welcome to Corporate Kindergarten. *Architectural Record*, 200(9), 36.
52 Schoeneman, D. (2006). Can Google Come Out to Play? *The New York Times*, 31 December. Available at: www.nytimes.com/2006/12/31/fashion/31google.html (Accessed: 5 May 2014).
53 Conley, D. (2009). *Elsewhere, USA: How we got from the company man, family dinners, and the affluent society to the home office, BlackBerry moms, and economic anxiety*. Random House LLC.
54 Baldry, C., and J. Hallier (2010). Welcome to the House of Fun: Workspace and Social Identity. *Economic and Industrial Democracy*, 31(1), 150-172.
55 Grubb, B. (2013). Do as we say, not as we do: Googlers don't telecommute. *The Sydney Morning Herald*, 19 February. Available at: www.smh.com.au/it-pro/business-it/do-as-we-say-not-as-we-do-googlers-dont-telecommute-20130218-2eo8w.html (Accessed: 5 May 2014).
56 Gorjan recently switched jobs and is now working for the Danish Technological Institute.
57 Constine, J. (2012). Cisco Acquires Enterprise Wi-Fi Startup Meraki For $1.2 Billion In Cash. *Techcrunch*, 18 November. Available at: http://techcrunch.com/2012/11/18/ (Accessed: 5 May 2014).

Flex offices

58 Ross, P. (2010). *Activity Based Working; The Hybrid Organisation: Buildings*. Available at: www.generation-e.com.au/attachments/article/188/Activity-based-working.pdf (Accessed: 20 May 2014).
59 Ross, P. (2012). Ten Predictions by Philip Ross, in: *Office wars 2012, A report by Orangebox into the changing workplace*. Available at: www.orangebox.com/downloads/smartworking_research/Boomers.pdf (Accessed: 20 May 2014).
60 Allen, T. J., and P.G. Gerstberger (1971). *Report of a field experiment to improve communications in a product engineering department; the non-territorial office*. Research report, MIT Sloan School of Management.
61 Ibid.
62 Ibid
63 Ibid.
64 Becker, F. (2005). *Offices at work: Uncommon workspace strategies that add value and improve performance*. John Wiley & Sons.
65 Quoted in: Berger, W. (1999). Lost in space. *Wired*, 7(2), 76-8l.
66 Berger, W. (1999). Lost in space. *Wired*, 7(2), 76-8l.
67 Becker, F. D., and Steele, F. (1995). *Workplace by design: Mapping the high-performance workscape*. Jossey-Bass.
68 Brown, G., Lawrence, T. B., and S.L. Robinson (2005). Territoriality in organizations. *Academy of Management Review*, 30(3), 577-594.
69 Hirst, A. (2011). Settlers, vagrants and mutual indifference: unintended consequences of hot-desking, *Journal of Organizational Change Management*, 24(6), 767-788

70　Hoendervanger, G.J., Been, I. De, Yperen, W. Van, and M.P. Mobach (2015). *Flexibility in use: Individual differences in the use and perception of activity-based office environments*. Center for People and Buildings (forthcoming).

71　Been, I. De and M. Beijer (2014). The influence of office type on satisfaction and perceived productivity support. *Journal of Facilities Management*, 12(2), 142-157.

72　Siri Blakstad was Telenor's head of workplace management until 2013. She is currently vice-president of the Norwegian engineering company Reinertsen

Studios

73　Wikipedia (2013). *Atelier*. Available at: http://en.wikipedia.org/wiki/Atelier (Accessed 17 May 2014)

74　Wikipedia (2012). *Studio*. Available at: http://en.wikipedia.org/wiki/Studio (Accessed 17 May 2014)

75　Isenberg, B. (2012). *Conversations with Frank Gehry*. Random House LLC.

76　Vyas, D., & Nijholt, A. (2012). Artful surfaces: an ethnographic study exploring the use of space in design studios. *Digital Creativity*, 23 (3-4), 176-195.

77　Schmidt, K., & Wagner, I. (2002). Coordinative Artifacts in Architectural Practise. *COOP*, 257-274

78　Isenberg, B. (2012). *Conversations with Frank Gehry*. Random House LLC.

79　Kirkham, P. (1990). Introducing Ray Eames. *Furniture History*, 26 (1990) 140.

80　Vyas, D., Nijholt, A., and G. van der Veer (2010). Supporting cooperative design through living artefacts. *Proceedings of the 6th Nordic Conference on Human-Computer Interaction: Extending Boundaries*, 541-550.

81　Heerwagen, J. H., Kampschroer, K., Powell, K. M., and V. Loftness (2004). Collaborative knowledge work environments. *Building Research & Information*, 32(6), 510-528.

82　Vohs, K. D., Redden, J. P., and R. Rahinel, (2013). Physical order produces healthy choices, generosity, and conventionality, whereas disorder produces creativity. *Psychological science*, 24(9), 1860-1867.

83　Florida, R. (2006). *The Flight of the Creative Class: The New Global Competition for Talent*. Liberal Education, 92(3), 22-29.

84　Underwood, M. (2006). Inside the Office of Charles and Ray Eames, *Ptah*, Aalto Foundation, Helsinki, 46-63.

85　Bernard, K. (2012). Studio Tour: Derek Lam's Workspace in SoHo. *Vogue*. Available at: www.vogue.com/vogue-daily/article/studio-visit-derek-lams-workspace-in-soho/#1 (Accessed 17 May 2014)

86　Jeziorek, P., Le Nart, A., Petruk, E. and B. Świątkowska (2010). *Creative People — Creative Living in Warsaw. Guide to Warsaw's Creative Sector*, The City of Warsaw

Modernist offices

87　Johnson, P. (1978). *Mies van der Rohe*. Secker & Warburg.

88　Quoted in: Lamster, M. (2013), A Personal Stamp on the Skyline. *The New York Times*. Available at: www.nytimes.com/2013/04/07/arts/design/building-seagram-phyllis-lamberts-new-architecture-book.html?pagewanted=all&_r=0 (Accessed: 27 August 2014).

89　Quoted in: Wright, G. (2008). *USA: Modern Architectures in History*. Reaktion books.

90　Budd, C. (2001). The office: 1950 to the present. In: Antonelli, P. (ed.). (2001). *Workspheres: Design and Contemporary Work Styles*. The Museum of Modern Art. 26-35.

91　De Botton, A. (2010). *The Pleasures and Sorrows of Work*. Random House LLC.

92　Budd, C. (2001). The office: 1950 to the present. In: Antonelli, P. (ed.). (2001). *Workspheres: Design and Contemporary Work Styles*. The Museum of Modern Art. 26-35.

93　De Botton, A. (2010). *The Pleasures and Sorrows of Work*. Random House LLC.

94　Betsky, A. (2011). The Apple HQ: Modernism on Valium. *Architect*. Available at: www.architectmagazine.com/blogs (Accessed: 27 Augustus 2014).

95　Duffy, F. and J. Tanis (1993), A Vision of the New Workplace. In: *Site Selection and Industrial Development*, April 1993

96　Florida, R. L. (2002). *The Rise of the Creative Class: And How It's Transforming Work, Leisure, Community and Everyday Life*. Basic Books.

97　Kersten, A., and R. Gilardi. 2003. The barren landscape: Reading US corporate architecture. In *Art and aesthetics at work*, ed. A. Carr and P. Hancock, 138–54. Basingstoke: Palgrave.

98　Saval, N. (2014). Cubed: A secret history of the workplace. Random House LLC.

99　Cornell University (date unknown), White Box. *The Interior Archetypes Research and Teaching Project*. Available at: www.intypes.cornell.edu (Accessed: 27 Augustus 2014).

100 Hine, T. (2000), Office Intrigues: The Interior Life of Corporate Culture. In: Albrecht, D. and C.B. Broikos (eds.) (2000). *On the job: Design and the American Office*. Princeton Architectural Press.

101 Betsky, A. (2011). The Apple HQ: Modernism on Valium, *Architect*. Available at: www.architectmagazine.com/blogs (Accessed: 27 Augustus 2014).

Process offices

102 Herman Miller (2009). *Call centers Find Their Voice*, Available at: www.hermanmiller.com/research/solution-essays/call-centers-find-their-voice.html (Accessed: 20 August 2014).

103 Callaghan, G. (2002). *Call centres -The Latest Industrial Office*. Presented at the 20th Annual International Labour Process Conference, Glasgow.

104 Haigh, G. (2012). *The Office: A Hardworking History*. The Miegunyah Press.

105 Meel, J. van (2000). *The European office: office design and national context*. 010 Publishers.
106 Beaufoy, S. (2007). *Slumdog millionaire*, draft for script, dated 4 November 2007.
107 Brophy, E. (2010). The subterranean stream: Communicative capitalism and call centre labour. *Ephemera: Theory and Politics in Organization*, 10(3/4), 470-483.
108 Herman Miller (2008). *New Directions in Call Center Design*. Available at: www.hermanmiller.com/content/dam/hermanmiller/documents/research_summaries/wp_Call_Center_Design.pdf (Accessed: 9 September 2014).
109 Ibid.
110 Ibid.
111 Zappos (2014). *Zappos Family Core Values*. Available at: http://about.zappos.com/our-unique-culture/zappos-core-values (Accessed: 9 September 2014).
112 Bloom, N., Liang, J., Roberts, J., and Z. J. Ying (2013). *Does Working from Home Work? Evidence from a Chinese Experiment (No. w18871)*. National Bureau of Economic Research.
113 Sykes Home (2014). *Your Day*. Available at: https://jobs.alpineaccess.com/day-in-the-life/your-day1/ (Accessed: 20 August 2014).
114 Sykes Home (2014). *Common Myths*. Available at: https://jobs.alpineaccess.com/work-home/work-home-overview/common-myths/ (Accessed: 9 September 2014).
115 The Economist (2013). The workforce in the cloud. *The Economist*. Available at: www.economist.com/news/business/21578658-talent-exchanges-web-are-starting-transform-world-work-workforce (Accessed: 9 September 2014).

Cell offices

116 Levin, G. (2007). *Edward Hopper, An Intimate Biography*. Random House Incorporated.
117 Veldhoen, E. (2004). *The Art of Working*. Academic Service.
118 Probst, R. (1968). *The Office: A Facility Based on Change*. Herman Miller Inc.
119 Quoted in: Duffy, F. C., Cave, C. and J. Worthington (eds.) (1976). *Planning Office Space*, Architectural Press.
120 Lake, A. (2013), The Way We Work. A Guide to Smart Working in Government. Available at: http://www.flexibility.co.uk/downloads/TW3-Guide-to-SmartWorking-withcasestudies-5mb.pdf (Accessed: 10 November 2014).
121 Kim, J., and R. de Dear (2013). Workspace satisfaction: The privacy-communication trade-off in open-plan offices. *Journal of Environmental Psychology*, 36, 18-26.
122 De Been, I., and M. Beijer (2014). The influence of office type on satisfaction and perceived productivity support. *Journal of Facilities Management*, 12(2), 142-157.
123 Pejtersen, J. H., Feveile, H., Christensen, K. B., & Burr, H. (2011). Sickness absence associated with shared and open-plan offices—a national cross sectional questionnaire survey. *Scandinavian Journal of Work Environment & Health*, 376-382.

124 Bodin Danielsson, C., Chungkham, H. S., Wulff, C., & Westerlund, H. (2014). Office design's impact on sick leave rates. *Ergonomics*, 57(2), 139-147.
125 IFMA (2010). *Space and Project Management Benchmarks, Research Report #34*. International Facility Management Association.
126 Oseland, N. (2013). Do lawyers still need private offices in the 21st Century? Why is open-plan so alien to many of them? *LinkedIn*. Group: Workplace Evolutionaries. Available at: www.linkedin.com/groups/Do-lawyers-still-need-private-4891376.S.252464396 (Accessed: 17 June 2014).
127 IFMA (2010). *Space and Project Management Benchmarks, Research Report #34*. International Facility Management Association.
128 Tangherlini, D. (2014). The Democracy of Space. *The GSA Blog*. Available at: http://gsablogs.gsa.gov/gsablog/2014/04/10/the-democracy-of-space/ (Accessed: 17 June 2014).
129 Armstrong, R. (2011). The Price of (Dev) Happiness: Part Two. Available at: http://blog.fogcreek.com/the-price-of-dev-happiness-part-two/ (Accessed: 17 June 2014).
130 Ibid.
131 Heerwagen, J. H., Kampschroer, K., Powell, K. M., and V. Loftness (2004). Collaborative knowledge work environments. *Building Research & Information*, 32(6), 510-528.
132 Cain, S. (2013). *Quiet: The Power of Introverts in a World That Can't Stop Talking*. Random House LLC.
133 van Meel, J., Martens, Y., & van Ree, H. J. (2010). *Planning office spaces: a practical guide for managers and designers*. Laurence King.

Recycled offices

134 Jonas Lang Lasalle (2014). *Global Market Perspective | Q3 2014*. Available at: www.jll.com/Research/JLL-Global-Market-Perspective-Q3-2014.pdf (Accessed: 8 September 2014).
135 Quoted in: Sherwin, A. (2012). Will we ever reach the Pinnacle? Skyscraper boom crashes to earth. *The Independent*, 19 November. Available at: www.independent.co.uk/arts-entertainment/architecture/will-we-ever-reach-the-pinnacle-skyscraper-boom-crashes-to-earth-8329216.html (Accessed: 5 June 2014).
136 Fried, J., & Hansson, D. H. (2013). Remote: Office Not Required. Random House LLC.
137 CoreNet Global (2013). Property Paradox: Space for Office Workers Continues to Decline, Even as Companies Expect Hiring to Increase in Months Ahead. Press release. Available at: www.corenetglobal.org/publications/newsdetail.cfm?Itemnumber=17990 (Accessed 9 September 2014).
138 Smith, A. and J. Anderson (2014), *AI, Robotics and the Future of Jobs*. Available at: www.pewinternet.org/files/2014/08/Future-of-AI-Robotics-and-Jobs.pdf (Accessed: 9 September 2014).

139 Frey, C. B., & Osborne, M. A. (2013). *The future of employment: how susceptible are jobs to computerisation?*. Available at: http://www. oxfordmartin.ox.ac.uk/downloads/academic/ The_Future_of_Employment.pdf(Accessed: 5 June 2014)

140 The Economist (2013). On 'bullshit jobs'. *The Economist*. Available at: http://www.economist. com/blogs/freeexchange/2013/08/labour-markets-0 (Accessed: 5 June 2014).

141 Toffler, A. (1981). *The Third Wave*. Pan Books.

142 Wikipedia (2011). *Adaptive reuse*. Available at: http://en.wikipedia.org/wiki/Adaptive_reuse (Accessed: 5 June 2014).

143 Remøy, H. T. (2010). *Out of Office: A Study on the Cause of Office Vacancy and Transformation as a Means to Cope and Prevent*. IOS Press.

Epilogue

144 Sailer, K., Budgen, A., Lonsdale, N., Turner, A. and A. Penn (2009). Evidence-Based Design: Theoretical and Practical Reflections of an Emerging Approach in Office Architecture. In: *Undisciplined!* Design Research Society Conference 2008, Sheffield Hallam University, Sheffield, 16-19 July 2008.

145 Duffy, F. (1974), *Office Interiors and Organizations*, PhD dissertation, Princeton University

146 Rapoport, A. (1969). *House, Form and Culture*. Foundations of Cultural Geography Series.

Image credits
For a small number of the images used in this book it proved impossible to identify the copyright holders. Such images have been assumed to belong to the public domain. If you claim ownership of any of these images and have not been properly identified, please notify the publisher and a formal acknowledgement will be made in future editions.

Image credits cover

Back   Front

Impact Hub, Amsterdam Courtesy of the Impact Hub	**Lego, Billund** Anders Sune Berg, Courtesy of Rosan Bosch	**Nykredit, Copenhagen** Adam Mørk, Courtesy of Schmidt hammer lassen architects	**Coffee Company, Rotterdam** Daria Scagliola & Stijn Brakkee	**Louise Scheele Elling, Remmarlöv** Peter Brinch	**Republikken, Copenhagen** Courtesy of Republikken
Gaaga Architecture, Leiden Marcel van der Burg, Courtesy of Gaaga Architecture	**McKinsey, Hong Kong** Philippe Ruault, Courtesy of OMA	**Next World, San Francisco** Mariko Reed, Courtesy of Jensen Architects	**Banco Santander, Querétaro** Rafael Gamo, Courtesy of Estudio Lamela	**Cisco Meraki, San Francisco** Jasper Sanidad, Courtesy of Studio O+A	**Park Theatre, London** Philip Vile, Courtesy of David Hughes Architects
GlaxoSmithKline, Philadelphia Alan Brian Nilsen, Courtesy of GSK	**Telenor, Fornebu** Espen Gees, Courtesy of Telenor	**DSM office, Sittard** Bram Vreugdenhil, Courtesy of Fokkema and Partners	**Noma Bar, London** Courtesy of Ecospace Studios	**Mutinerie, Paris** Stefano Borghi, Courtesy of Mutinerie	**MAD Architects, Beijing** Alessandro Digaetano
Teletech, Dijon Philippe Ruault, Courtesy of MVRDV	**Customer Service Centre CBA, Melbourne** James Newman, Courtesy of Frost* Design	**Mamastudio, Warshaw** Courtesy of Mamastudio	**Derek Lam, New York** Dean Kaufman, Courtesy of SO-IL	**Bigelow Laboratory for Ocean Sciences, Maine** Christopher Barnes, Courtesy of Perkins + Will	**Google, Dublin** Peter Würmli, Courtesy of Camenzind Evolution

About the author
Juriaan van Meel is co-founder of ICOP, an international
consultancy firm based in the Netherlands and
Denmark. He is also a senior researcher at the Centre
for Facilities Management at the Danish Technical
University. His publications include books such as *The
European Office* and *Planning Office Spaces: a practical
guide for managers and designers*. Both as an advisor
and researcher, Juriaan studies the changing nature
of work and workplaces and how these changes can be
translated into better buildings and interiors.
Juriaan's own work takes place at a shared desk at the
Danish Technical University, any available spot at the
ICOP office in Rotterdam, the kitchen table at his home
in Copenhagen, and the many spaces in between.

© Juriaan van Meel

Centre for Facilities Management - Realdania Research
Technical University of Denmark
www.cfm.dtu.dk

Credits
Text and illustrations by Juriaan van Meel
Book design by Sander Boon
Copy editing by Robyn Dalziel
Research funded by Realdania
Published by ICOP/Centre for Facilities Management
Printed by Pantheon Drukkers, Amstelveen
Binding by Van Waarden, Zaandam

ISBN 978-90-823479-0-6